W9-BYZ-786

STRIP CUTS

STRIP CUTS

DAVID DRAYER

ROWDY HOUSE PUBLISHING

Copyright © 2000 by David Drayer

This book is a work of fiction. Names, characters, places and incidents are products of the author's imagination or are used fictitiously. Any resemblance to actual events or locales, or persons, living or dead, is entirely coincidental.

All rights reserved. Printed and bound in the United States of America. No part of this book may be reproduced or transmitted in any form or by any means, electronic or mechanical, including photocopying, recording, or by an information storage and retrieval system except by a reviewer who may quote brief passages in a review to be printed in a magazine or newspaper, without permission in writing from the publisher. For information, please contact Rowdy House Publishing, P.O. Box 251293, Los Angeles, California 90025.

First printing 2000.

"The Smell of Snow" was originally published in the
Palo Alto Review, Fall 1999.

Library of Congress Cataloging-in-Publication Data
Drayer, David.
Strip cuts / by David Drayer. — 1st ed.
p. cm.
LCCN: 99-67197
ISBN: 0-9675215-6-4
1. Pennsylvania—Fiction. 2. Cities and towns
—Pennsylvania—Fiction. I. Title.
PS3554.R288S77 2000   813'.54
QBI99-1446

Book Design: Terry Klann
Landscape Photography: Jeanne Drayer

For Sue
Who always takes me higher

and

For Dad, Mom, Sis, and Toot
Who inspire me in everything I do

ACKNOWLEDGMENTS

Thanks to Jean and Sy for letting me hang my hat in the "bowling alley" where many of these stories were written; to Donna, Brian, and Chuck for their early and unwavering support; and to Terry and Dora for their faith, talent, time, and most of all, friendship.

strip cut (strip kut), *n.* 1. a piece of land that has been strip-mined for coal. 2. barren land.

CONTENTS

Welcome to

CHERRY RUN, PENNSYLVANIA

THE KING GAME

When your nickname is Jack-Off and you're stuck in Cherry Run, life really bites.

That's what I should have told Bernie when he was strutting around asking me what I had to say for myself. "It's hard, Mr. Kavanaugh," I could have said with a little quiver in my voice. A tear would have been overkill, but a little quiver would have been nice. "There's no place for me. Making up the King Game was my way of having fun, I guess, for the first time since high school started."

Who am I kidding? It wouldn't have mattered. Bernie would have done the same damn thing: sat there, hands folded, not listening to a word I said, thinking of big words to make me feel stupid, and then giving me three days in-school detention. He loves it. He would have given me the board if he thought he could get away with it. Bernie was famous for his swats. He called his paddle "The Communicator" and made a real show out of using it.

Dad would kick old Bernie's ass if he ever tried that with me again. He damn near broke the board over me last year for fighting in gym class, and I didn't even start the fight. My dad got wind of it, and the next thing I knew we were in the truck heading to Bernie's house. Dad was madder at Bernie than he was at me.

Bernie's house was pretty fancy and he was still dressed in his black suit when he opened the door. I felt so weird being there, I could hardly stand to look at him. Not Dad. He went in there as big as you please. Old Earl Hardy in his work clothes and steel-toed boots. His hands were rougher than a corncob and still filthy from the mines. He told Bernie, "I know my boy is no angel. And you got a hell of a job trying to keep order, but I don't stand for anyone hitting my kids. I'd think a man in your position would know that smacking a thirteen-year-old kid don't do much good anyway. It does little more than piss them off."

I couldn't believe Dad said "piss them off" to Bernie.

"There are other forms of discipline," he said, "and when my boy steps out of line, you use any of them you see fit. And if that don't work, you call me and I'll handle it."

Bernie acted real concerned, saying, "I see. Well, I completely respect your opinions, Mr. Hardy." And shit like that. He was nice as pie. Nothing like the dick he is in school. Dad was glad everything went smooth, though. I think he was kind of proud of himself. Not that Bernie fooled him.

He knows Bernie's an asshole. Bernard Allan Kavanaugh, smiling in this week's newspaper beside the president of the Mothers Against Drunk Driving. Like the phony bastard didn't get picked up last summer drunker than a skunk. Everyone knows. There's no proof, of course, because Jeff Cohen's old man, the town cop, let him go. Which is nothing new. His old man never arrests anyone who can do something for him. Doctors, dentists, store owners, and big people at the school are pretty safe, but Cohen's old man makes them sweat for a while, anyway. Jeff told the homeroom class about it and it spread from there. He said Bernie was almost bawling and begging not to be written up.

Dang near everybody in this town hits the bottle. Why not the high school principal? I don't, and I'm proud of it too. I'm not a goody-two-shoes or anything, but I've got to keep my wits about me. I don't want to end up like the losers that hang at the bars. They're trapped here forever. The day I turn eighteen, I'm hitting the road.

Besides, there's not much opportunity to drink if you don't go to parties. No one is going to invite a guy named Jack-Off to their party except to make him the butt of all jokes. Screw that. I'd rather be alone.

"I forgot you were here." Mrs. Miller sticks her pointy, freckled face around the door.

"Yeah."

She looks at me like dog crap on the bottom of her shoe. "Well, after three days of this maybe you'll learn a little respect."

"Yeah." She walks away. "Screw you."

"Excuse me?"

I can tell by her look she didn't really hear.

"I have to leave at 2:00."

"Detention goes until 2:55."

"But I'm on the Worker's Early Release."

"Not for the next three days you're not."

"Bern—Mr. Kavanaugh didn't say anything to me about that."

She shuts the door. What a bitch. The only thing I learn around here are new ways to keep from getting depressed.

And what I come up with always gets me in trouble—like the King Game. Detention isn't so bad. I don't mind being by myself. The morning flew by. I was working on my short story for English class.

Now that class, I miss: Candy Bracknell up there telling us about Hemingway and Fitzgerald with her long blonde hair. She's wearing the blue dress today too. It's a tight fit and her nipples show through the fabric.

Man, I could get a boner just thinking about it. It bites to get a boner in her class, which I do damn near every day. A boner in detention isn't so bad. It's kind of fun, actually.

I wonder what Candy thinks when she hears those assholes call me Jack-Off. She pretends not to hear, but I know she does.

When people call you Jack-Off, that's all you are to them. A jack-off, a screw-up, a nothing. Some people take it the other way and assume that I jack off all the time because I can't get any girlfriends, which I can't, because in Cherry Run if you're not part of the "in" crowd, you can pretty much forget it. That doesn't leave a guy anything but his imagination…and his hand. Still, that doesn't have diddly dick to do with how I got the nickname.

During shop class in seventh grade old Bug Eyes was absent and we had a substitute. I was sitting on one of the tables staring out the window, wishing I was somewhere else, and he points at me and says, "Jack!" then snaps his fingers and points at the floor, "Off!"

His face turned red as a beet and he tried to fix it by adding, "Off the table. Get off the table." But it was too late. The Jocks already got a hold of it, and they were laughing their asses off. Just like that, my entire high school existence was screwed. And to top it off, Jack isn't even my name. The nimrod called me by the wrong damn name.

Back then, I still had faith. I thought Cherry Run was an okay place and that high school would be, like my dad always said, "the best years of life."

Yeah right.

I was really upset about the nickname. Being the wide-eyed idiot that I was, I went to my dad for advice on what to do about it. Just the thought makes me cringe. Stupid, stupid, stupid!

Poor Dad seemed surprised at the question. He was the kind of guy who never had a problem like that, and I probably killed all the visions he had for me. He did a pretty good job of covering up his disappointment and gave me some advice. It boiled down to three options:

1) Ignore them.

I'd been using that one already and it didn't work for shit.

2) Bust them a good one.

That one sounded great in theory and I had hundreds of fantasies about it. But there was no way. Practically everyone called me that and most of them were bigger than me. Getting beat up would have just made things worse. And it would hurt too.

3) Prove them wrong.

The choice was obvious.

I tried out for the football team the summer between seventh and eighth grade. When they told me to come in for my uniform, I damn near peed my pants with excitement. I told my dad about how I made the team. I went to school and bragged to anyone who would listen, while Dad must have gone to work and done the same thing. We both soon found out that everyone made it. It was more of a sign-up than a tryout.

That should have told me right there to forget it, but I was too busy modeling the shoulder pads and stretching the hell out of one of Dad's old tee shirts. I looked huge. While I was modeling, I smudged some of Dad's shoe polish under my eyes to imitate that black stuff the Steelers wear for Sunday football games.

The jersey was my favorite thing though. I got to pick whichever one I wanted out of a musty, wrinkled pile. I took the biggest number I could find: 99. I was so psyched that I ignored the league name, Pee-Wee, as well as the fact that I didn't know shit about how to play the game.

I was sure that jersey would change my life. I wore it everywhere. And for a while, people did treat me differently. Grown men even talked to me: "How's the team this year?" or "Are you guys going to kick some butt down in East Brady?" And every now and then some asshole would say, "A little small for football, ain't you?"

My dad overheard one of those remarks and said, "You tell them, 'Dynamite comes in a small package.'"

Yeah, right, Dad, I'm going to say that. Even then, full of hope, I knew I wasn't dynamite. An M-80 maybe, but that's about it.

It reminded me of my Uncle George's Sunday School class. If anyone got to feeling down on themselves he'd say, "Don't worry. God don't make junk." He told us that God gave everyone something special. A gift. I started dreaming that mine was football. I saw myself strutting on the sideline, hair wet with sweat, gulping a Gatorade. But Uncle George also said that God worked in mysterious ways and that it wasn't our place to question Him.

I should have known I was screwed.

All I really knew about football was that the object was to get the ball over the goal line and that the other team would try to stop you. Actually, I still don't know much more than that.

Dan Moss, the math teacher, was our coach. Everybody

called him "Big Dan," even though he was short. He was pretty stocky though, and always warned us not to get smart with him. He didn't have much to worry about with our crew.

Football turned out to be just like everything else. Other people decided who I got to be. They pegged old 99 as a bench-warmer right from the word go. They never even gave me the basics of the game. I was at every single practice, but the coaches sent me and the other scrubs off to run laps or hit the pads while they did their real coaching with the first-stringers.

Pee-Wee football was serious business to Big Dan, and he wasn't about to waste time with scrubs who would never get to play anyway. He threw a fit every time we lost: ranting and raving, hitting things. It pissed me off even then. It sure as hell wasn't my fault. And then there was Joey Knight, our quarterback. He cried every time we lost. I thought that was a bit much. His old man used to be a star quarterback at Cherry Run, and Joey was on the starting team, so it was okay for him to cry. Big Dan once pointed at Joey and said, "It's nice to know that someone gives a damn about this team."

A couple of guys tried to work up some tears after that but it didn't pan out. Stevie Myers cried once, but he was a bench-warmer like me and his old man was never anybody in school. Big Dan told him to grow up.

The season was more than halfway over when I finally got in. Even at halftime everyone knew the game was won. Big Dan was all smiles. The assistant coach, a guy who always looked tired and never smiled, handed out Hershey's chocolate bars to keep our energy up. He made a face at me when I picked up my candy bar because I hadn't played yet that season. I figured screw him— if they're handing out free candy bars, I'm getting one.

By the fourth quarter, we were beating the Clarion Bobcats 44 to 6. Joey Knight said, "Even you'll get to play today."

And he'd get to go home with dry eyes, the bawl-baby.

With five minutes left on the clock, Big Dan walked down my way. "Has everyone been in?" he said.

Stevie Myers and I looked at each other and then shot our hands up in the air. Big Dan slapped my helmet. "You go in as right tackle on offense."

I stared at him.

"Take Carson's place."

I took off and he grabbed my jersey. "Whoa! Wait until the play is over."

I thought it was a real waste that they never put me in all season because I got past my man every single time and was up the field, wide open, waving my arms for Ray Peters, the third-string quarterback, to throw me the ball. "Peters!" I shouted. I had flashes of snagging the ball out of the air and taking it all the way. Three times in a row I was open and Peters never threw it to me. Two of the three times the jerk got sacked.

The next thing I knew I was back on the bench. That was it for me. Three plays. All those damn practices for three plays. Knight was laughing, shaking his head, helmet off, the big hero. "What the hell were you doing out there, man?"

"Getting open," I said, as indignant as hell, tearing off my helmet. "It's not my fault he didn't throw me the ball."

"He's not supposed to throw you the ball, dip-shit. You went in as right tackle."

"On offense," I said. My face was burning up.

"No shit. You were supposed to be *guarding* him. Why do you think he got sacked?"

Why the hell was that the first time I ever heard that a right tackle, even if he's on offense, is supposed to guard the quarterback? And why did I have to hear it from Knight?

I never fought so hard to hold back tears in my life. I felt like such an asshole. A jack-off. But I wasn't going to give those Jocks the last laugh. No way. I just shrugged my padded shoulders and acted like I didn't care.

Stevie Myers went in as a receiver. I watched as he got open and Peters threw him the ball. He caught it and off he went in the direction of our goal line. No one, including me, knew how fast Stevie could run. He zipped up the field, beating everyone, spiked the ball, and did a dance like the Steelers do on TV. He was waving his hands and jerking like a chicken.

Big Dan was screaming, "YOU—DIDN'T—CROSS—THE—GOAL—LINE!"

Poor Stevie didn't know what the hell was going on when one of the Bobcats knocked him on his ass right in the middle of his dance and another one picked up the ball and took it to the other end of the field.

Everyone laughed at him. Even Big Dan laughed because there was no way we were going to lose the game over it. And it still pisses me off that I laughed at him too. I joined in on razzing him on the bus ride home. Stevie was the only friend I had on the whole football team and I abandoned him that day too. He made a bigger ass out of himself than I did, so I got to slip in with the others.

I had planned to tell him I was sorry about that, but I never did.

Two weeks later, we played Cherry Run's all-time rivals, the East Brady Bulldogs, and I'm happy to say that they whipped our asses. At halftime it was already 24 to zip. Big Dan was fit to be tied. There were rumors that he bet a lot of money on the game but there was no way of ever really knowing. I'm sure it's true though, because I'd never seen him so mad. The locker room was very quiet. I looked as sad as everybody else on the outside, but on the inside I was loving it. Besides, it wasn't my fault these dickheads were getting beat. For me, football had become nothing but a bus ride to different schools where I could check out the cheerleaders. At that age, you could almost see their boobs growing.

Anyway, Big Dan walked in and the guys were barely breathing so as not to make any noise. The only sound was Joey Knight whimpering with his face buried in his arms. Big Dan stood in front of us with his hands on his hips and his head hung low. Then, out of nowhere, he spun around and slammed his fist into the washing machine. Everyone jumped and Joey gasped.

"Are you losers?" He looked right at us. His eyes were all buggy and bloodshot. "Are you? I don't know about you, but I am ashamed to go out there and show my face."

I hated him. I hated all those bastards and I wanted revenge. For me. For Stevie. And I was going to get it.

That place was silent and I mean *silent.*

And then.

A fart.

It squealed out of my ass, sharp and high-pitched. The fart of an angry clown. At that moment in time, any fart was bad news, but this one was villainous. Everyone seemed frozen as the sound bounced off the lockers and the walls of the shower. It was beautiful. A couple of guys burst out laughing before the echo was even gone and then the room exploded with everybody blaming everybody else. Pushing each other, hitting each other. I was blaming people too, but I was bursting inside. They didn't even know it was me. I was a free man. A kamikaze who somehow got to walk away! Scot-free!

And just as quickly as the room got noisy, it got quiet again. Everyone turned to Big Dan with a look of horror. A look that said, "It wasn't me!" His face was almost purple. He looked like he was going to explode.

"Who did that?" he almost whispered.

His head snapped from side to side. "I'm asking you a question." He started to skulk around the room, his arms out from his body like an ape. "What's the matter? Haven't you got the guts to admit it?" Then he threw his clipboard. Everyone ducked as it crashed into the lockers barely above our heads. "I try to teach you snot-nosed little bastards something about winning, something about pride, and this is what I get: a room full of farting hogs."

Big Dan made us run a lot of extra laps at the next practice. If Peters wouldn't have thrown up, we'd probably still be running. A few guys figured out that the unknown farter had to be me. I denied it up and down. I'm a great liar. I never used to lie. I was so honest it was stupid. I still don't like to lie most of the time, but it doesn't matter with these assholes. I tell them lies just like I used to tell them the truth, and I'm better off for it.

They said if they ever found out it was me, they'd give me a swirly. Bullshit. If they ever stuck my head down the commode, I'd shoot them with my deer rifle. And that's no lie.

It's 1:00 and I should be leaving for work in an hour. I can't believe Bernie didn't tell me I had to stay till 2:55. What a dick. They're going to have a fit when I show up at the farm an hour late. Mrs. Miller opens the door and in walks Dean Smith and Chopper Gutterson. "Wait here until Mr. Kavanaugh calls you in," she says to them and shuts the door.

Chopper's face is red and there's a bloody scratch on his neck. He socks himself down in the chair so hard I can feel it through the floor. Dean sits down on the other side of me. Away from Chopper. He sits hunched forward with his arms on his thighs. He stares at the floor.

Chop keeps sighing and looking over. I look at my watch and act like I'm deep in thought. Dean doesn't move.

"Fucking Wire Head," Chop hisses at Dean. They call him that because of his kinky, red hair. Actually, he looks more like an orange Q-Tip to me, but I've got nothing against Dean.

"You are fucking dead! Wiry-headed prick," Chopper says, and a piece of spit flies out of his mouth and lands on my arm. We both look at it and then look at each other. I wipe it off casually.

"Hey Jack-Off," Chopper says to me, "you know you're sitting next to a dead man? I got a lot of cousins in this town. I got a lot of fucking cousins, man."

He does, and they're all assholes like him. They're always fighting. "You're dead!" is their favorite expression, but they've never killed anyone that I know of. Chopper's old man really was killed though, in a bar fight at the Ruffled Grouse. We were just kids. I remember Chop didn't come to school for weeks. My dad told me it was a shame for the guy who went to prison for it because it was an accident and Chopper's old man had it coming.

The door opens again and this time it's Bernie. He looks us over like he's a cop in some movie and we're the criminals. Mrs. Miller is behind him. There was a rumor that they had an affair together even though they are both married. I couldn't picture either one of them naked, let alone screwing. The next time I get a boner in Candy's class, all I need to do to get rid of it is think of these two pounding away.

"What do we have here? The Three Stooges?" Bernie says. Mrs. Miller laughs through her nose and that just puffs him up even more. He loves this shit.

"A newcomer and a regular," she says, as though we aren't in the room with them.

Dean is the newcomer and Chopper is the regular.

"Jake and Dean were fighting in gym class."

"I'm surprised at you, Dean," Bernie said.

Dean looks up at him all wide-eyed. "Mr. Kavanaugh, I—"

"Save it. You'll both have a chance to talk." He turns to Mrs. Miller and says, "I've got to make a quick call, then you can send the boxers in."

"Mr. Kavanaugh," I said. "I have to leave at 2:00."

"Detention goes until 2:55, and if I hear another word about it, I'll take you off the Worker's Early Release Program for the year."

What a dick. The job's not that big of a deal. I help out at Anderson's farm a couple of hours after school for minimum wage. Getting out of school early is the real reason I took the job.

When Dean and Chopper go in, Dean doesn't shut the door behind them. I can hear everything. Bernie goes through his usual shit of how this school is to be respected, and as long as he is at the helm, misconduct will not be tolerated.

Then he lets Chopper talk.

"We weren't fighting," Chop says in a jolly voice I've never heard him use before.

"Really," Bernie says. "How did you get that scratch?"

"Dean and me—"

"Dean and I."

"Yeah. Dean and I were just fooling around. We were just kidding with each other and it got a little rough, I guess. Weren't we Dean?"

Silence.

"Is that true, Dean?" Bernie asks.

"No." Dean sounds upset. His voice is quiet and kind of shaky. "He's been calling me names and pushing me around for weeks. I'm sick of it. I didn't do a damn thing to him."

"Watch your language, mister."

Chop jumps in. "I was just joking with you. We were all kidding."

"Were you kidding when you pulled my hair? When you knocked me into the lockers? You and your asshole group."

"I'm not going to warn you about your language again," Bernie says, like he thinks he's Clint Eastwood.

"You were laughing about it." Chop is scrambling now. He's not used to this kind of honesty, I'm sure.

"You liar!" It sounds like Dean is crying.

"Alright, now!" Bernie says. "What's the truth?"

"The truth is I have been picked on and called names and pushed around and I'm sick and tired of it. I never did anything to them. I can't stand it anymore. I hit him and he deserved it. If he does it again—"

"Alright, alright," Bernie sighs. "Now look, Dean. If you are telling me that Jake was picking on you and the two of you were indeed fighting, then I'm going to have to punish both of you."

"But he started it." Dean is really upset. I can't believe it.

"It takes two to fight." That's one of Bernie's favorite lines and he used it on me last year. It's bullshit. He says, "Now, I'm going to ask you once more: Were you kidding, because if you were, I'll let you go with a warning. Or were you fighting?"

"We were kidding," Chop says.

"I'm asking Dean."

"He was picking on me. I didn't do anything to him and he picked on me until I couldn't stand it. And as soon as we leave here, he's going to keep right on doing it."

"He's a liar," Chop says.

"Mr. Kavanaugh, I'm tired of taking his shit and I shouldn't have to—"

"That's it. It's settled then. Jake, you will both spend the weekend doing writing assignments, and since Dean doesn't know how to control his mouth, he gets an extra one."

"It's not fair," Dean says.

"Do you want a third?"

Chop wants to know if he can take swats instead.

"No, Jake, you can't take swats. After as many as you've had, I think you've developed an immunity." Then there's this long pause and Bernie says, and I can hear the smile on his face, "However, Dean here has the option of swats. What do you say, Dean?"

He doesn't answer.

"I'll assume you want the board if you don't answer."

"Writing," Dean says.

Chopper chuckles at this.

"Very well. The assignments can be picked up from Mrs. Miller tomorrow morning and they will be due Monday morning. Good afternoon, gentlemen."

They leave and Chop looks like he's itching to tell Dean that he's going to be dead. Poor Dean. He's in deep now. He must have thought that Bernie was going to help him the way he was spouting the truth in there. Instead, he gets two writing assignments and the wrath of Chopper and all his asshole cousins.

"King Seth, I presume," Candy says.

She's standing in the doorway holding a bunch of papers. My heart starts racing and my face gets red. I can't think of anything to say so I just smile. Blue dress. Blonde hair. Nipples. I look at her face. Beautiful face. How long did I look at her nipples? Probably too long. She probably thinks I'm a pervert. I can feel how red my face is. I'm getting a boner.

"How did you know about the king stuff?" I get the words out just in time. My mouth goes cotton dry and I swallow hard.

"I have my ways." She likes me. I love her. "My best pupil is in detention. How can I explain that one?"

I've got a solid A in English. I'm pretty much C's in everything else. I shrug my shoulders and give her the biggest, stupidest smile she's probably ever seen.

"Well, detention or not, your short story is due Monday."

"I'm almost done," I gush out like an idiot.

"I look forward to reading it," and she's gone. The door is still open and I see her hand the papers to Mrs. Miller and then go.

I wonder how much she knows about the King Game. Someday, when I'm out of this damn school, I'd like to tell her about it in full detail. She'd love it. But she couldn't let on now. Because she's a teacher, she has to act like it's a terrible thing and I shouldn't have done it.

King Seth, she called me. King Seth.

King. We've been studying King David in Uncle George's Sunday School class. My boner starts to shrink at the thought. Boners and Sunday School *do not* go together.

Old King David was pretty cool as far as Bible people go. Uncle George said that David took all the guys no one wanted and made a mighty army. An unbeatable army all made up of scrubs. That's sort of what I did. Sort of. Of course, David did it for God. God probably wouldn't be too pleased with me.

My army is, or was, I guess, Pooch and Carl. Pooch is the biggest kid in our class. He's already six feet tall and weighs over two hundred pounds. The football coaches tried to get him to join the team but he didn't want anything to do with it. His family lives out in the boonies; his old man is a poacher, but since they eat everything they shoot, the game wardens kind of look the other way. There are rumors that they even shoot and eat stray dogs. I don't think it's true, but his dad ended up with the nickname Dog. Sure enough, the son of Dog is Pooch.

Carl is like the opposite of Pooch now that I think about it. He's a scrawny little guy with thick, black hair that hangs in his eyes. I don't know if he has some kind of problem or what, but his hands shake all the time. Pooch and me let on like we don't notice it. A lot of the other kids pick on him though, calling him Shaky and shit like that.

The game was simple: The king makes up dares for the subjects to do. The king decides how many points each dare is worth. Whichever subject gets one thousand points first becomes the new king.

Since I made up the game, I got to be king first. It was the most fun I ever had in school. Well worth detention. I started Pooch and Carl out on simple dares at first: making funny noises in class, shooting paper wads, little things. And they got hooked. We all were hooked. It was like gambling or something. Pooch had forty points, then Carl had forty-five, then Pooch went for fifty.

And then we got serious. Carl ate his lunch standing on his chair in the lunchroom. When Mrs. Getty, who looks a lot like a monkey, told him to get down, he ignored her.

"Carl!" she said. Her face was red and so was Carl's as he stood there munching on a pizza burger. Everyone was looking and wondering what the hell, but the longer Carl stayed up there the more points he got. "I'm not going to tell you again!"

Pooch was sweating it out. He kept whispering in my ear, "How many's he got? How many now?"

Poor Mrs. Getty grabbed Carl's shirt and started tugging at him. Carl wobbled, looked at me and I mouthed, "Thirty points!" He held his ground. The whole damn cafeteria was watching and Carl wanted to stop but he was getting a point a second from the time Mrs. Getty first told him to get down.

"This ain't fair," Pooch said. "There has to be a cut-off point."

"Bullshit, Pooch, a deal's a deal."

"Give me something to do."

I looked at Mrs. Getty's red face and I whispered to Pooch, "Go up, right now, and tell her she looks like a monkey."

"No fucking way."

"Fine."

"How many points has he got?"

"Ninety and counting."

"No fucking way," Pooch said. "How much for calling her a monkey?"

"Seventy-five."

"To her face? No way!"

Then Pooch jumped out of his seat and laid a hand on Mrs. Getty's shoulder and said, "You look like a monkey. You have a monkey—"

She grabbed him by the ear, bent him in half, and pulled him across the cafeteria all the way to the office. The cafeteria cheered. Carl ended up with 120 points. Pooch negotiated for an extra twenty-five since he went to the office by his ear and took three swats after he got there.

By then the whole school wanted to know what we were up to. But part of the deal was, from the beginning, it was our secret. No one was to be told. It was fun at first, but people really wanted to know and we were getting major shit from people for not saying. It was the worst when the Jocks wanted to know. No one says no to the Jocks. Those guys are the stars of the school. They go with the girls we fantasize about. They would normally never think of talking to us, but there they were, sitting at our table, asking us about the game.

We didn't say. Carl would have if it weren't for Pooch and me. Pooch hated the bastards as much as I did. We tried to be funny in our answers, but it just pissed them off. Gym class was a damn nightmare. Especially Dodge Ball games. Last gym class, when we played, someone caught my ball so I was out early in the game. I was sitting on the side up against the wall when a ball slammed into my face and bounced my head off the brick wall. Everything went black and I saw a spark. Things got bleary, but when I could see again, everyone was laughing at me. Joey Knight was the one. "Oops," he said. "That one must have slipped."

I wasn't bawling, but my eyes were watering like hell. Knight said, "Ah, don't cry Jack-Off, it was just an accident."

Mr. Henderson, the gym teacher, is also the varsity basketball coach. He was laughing too. Then he looked at Knight and said, "That's enough, Knight."

"It slipped."

"If it slips again, you'll have to sit out the rest of the period."

My head hurt for two days after that. Dad would have raised hell if he knew, but I wouldn't tell him. It was bad enough that his only boy was known as Jack-Off. Why tell him that I get pushed around on top of it? Besides, I had a much better idea.

I called a secret conference with Pooch and Carl while we were waiting for the bus. I'd come up with the best dare yet: three hundred points.

Pooch shook his head. "No fucking way, man. No fuck-ing way!"

"You're crazy," Carl said, running a shaky hand through his hair. "You must think we're stupid."

"Three hundred points! That would put either one of you near the nine hundred mark. A day or two after that, one of you would be the new king. You could come up with these wild-assed dares, and I'd have to do them."

"This one should be instant king," Pooch said.

"It shouldn't be a dare at all," Carl said. "That's serious business. You could go to jail for that."

"Not if they didn't know who did it," I said. "You guys are afraid. I can't believe it. After the dares you guys have pulled off in the last week, I figured nothing was too big."

"This is fucking suicide," Pooch said.

"Come on, he's got it coming." They weren't budging. So I thought about it. "Okay. You guys can split the dare. One hundred and fifty points a piece."

"Forget it," Carl said.

After Carl's bus left, I worked on Pooch. We were cracking up at how funny it would be. "Picture it," I said, laughing like a damned hyena. "Big man Knight driving his Camaro smelling like he went swimming in a vat of piss."

"I know what would be better," Pooch said.

"What could be better than taking a piss all over Knight's plush bucket seats?"

Pooch leaned in. "Sprinkling a little fox piss on them."

"Huh?" I imagined him holding a fox inside Knight's car and waiting for it to pee. We cracked up.

"No, you fucker!" Pooch said. Him and his dad were trappers. They lured a fox to the trap by sprinkling fox urine around the area. You can buy a bottle of the stuff at hunting and trapping places. "It wouldn't take much," he said. "My old man got a couple of drops on his hands once." Pooch twisted up his face and shook his head. "Oo-wee, did that stink. It's worse than anything. It's way worse than shit. It makes human shit smell like roses. And the fucking stuff had to wear off. You can't wash it off. He stunk for a week. And that was just a few drops."

"Imagine what a whole bottle would do."

"No way, I couldn't even imagine a whole bottle."

I really wanted it and Pooch said he'd do it, *if* he were instant king.

"I can't do that!"

"The fuck you can't. You're the king."

"Carl would have a fit. He's not even here."

"Then forget it."

"How many points do you have now?"

"Five hundred and forty."

"I'll give you three hundred and sixty. That will give you an even nine hundred."

"Nope."

"Come on. You'll beat Carl then for sure and he won't be as pissed. Come on, man. If I make you instant king, he might quit."

Pooch loved the game as much as I did, and he wanted his turn at king. He thought about it. I made myself be quiet while he thought. Then he said, "You have to pay for the piss."

"I'll do it."

"It's expensive."

"I don't care. How much?"

"About eight bucks for a little bottle."

"Eight bucks! For a bottle of pee?" What the hell. It would be worth it. I had some money from my job at Anderson's. "Fine. I'll pay for it."

After work, we caught a ride to the Rod and Gun Shop in Rimersburg and got the stuff. It wasn't unusual for him to buy trapping supplies there. He brought trapper gloves from home

and when we got about a mile from Knight's house, we split
up. They lived right on the edge of Cherry Run in a huge brick
house. No close neighbors. Perfect. Pooch went by himself and
planned to meet me in the cemetery when the job was done.

About forty-five minutes later, he came tearing up
through the dark cemetery, scaring the hell out of me. He was
grinning ear to ear. "Nine hundred points! Nine hundred
fucking points!"

"How'd you get in the car? Was it unlocked?"

"Unlocked! The jockstrap had the damned window
halfway down. I didn't even have to open the door."

"How do I know you really did it?"

He was laughing like a drunk. "You'll know. You'll know."

"Where's the gloves and the bottle?"

"I threw them in the creek. You got to buy me new gloves
so my old man doesn't find out mine are missing."

"Why'd you pitch 'em?

"They were covered, man. Everything in that car was
covered. The seats, the carpet."

I would have bought him fifty new pairs of gloves at that
moment. I'd work at Anderson's Farm for no other reason than
to buy old Pooch gloves!

We took the woods home, cracking up like crazy about it.
Pooch almost fell in the creek laughing when he imagined the
gloves and bottle floating by. The next day we told Carl. He
was mad.

"It doesn't count. I wasn't there."

"The fuck it doesn't," Pooch said. Then he exaggerated a
big smile at Carl. "Nine-zero-zero!"

Knight never made it to school that day. Neither did
the three other Jocks who rode with him. They didn't know
what happened. Since the window was down that night,

they figured that a cat or something got in and made a mess. The whole school was talking about it. Poor Joey, kids were saying, he loves that car.

I called a private conference with Pooch and Carl and we laughed until tears were dropping off our faces. We were stumbling around like drunks, falling over each other, slapping each other on the back, picturing the scene.

Pooch made a sniffing sound and said, "Do you guys smell something?"

We were dying. Carl's face looked like a cherry tomato. "Who farted?" he said, imitating what one of the Jocks might have said.

My stomach hurt so bad I thought I'd get sick. Old Bug Eyes, the shop teacher, asked us what we were up to, and we lost it all over again. Right before Carl's bus came, we agreed to lay low for a week or two. "Don't mention anything to anyone, and no more dares for a while. We can't afford to call attention to ourselves," I said, knocking a tear from my face and swallowing another laugh. "Seriously."

Carl gave Pooch a punch on the arm and told him that he deserved the nine hundred points, and then he winked like he was imitating a movie star and said, "But the game's not over yet."

We got the whole story over the next week and a half. Every time one of us heard a chunk of it, we called a conference. The Jocks who rode with Knight that morning had to burn their clothes. Even soaking in tomato soup didn't get the smell completely out of their skin. The dumb asses thought that maybe it wasn't a cat after all, but some kind of a skunk. This stuff was way worse than skunk. Anyway, they had the car professionally cleaned and it still didn't work. His parents actually put the damn thing up for sale, and big bad Joey Knight bawled like a baby.

It was the best, and still, no one but us knew about it. The King Game was going full speed ahead until we had a substitute teacher for homeroom.

That's what sunk us.

By that time, the story was cooling off and we were all itching to get back to the game. School was horrible without it. And Carl was all pumped up about tying the score.

The substitute was Mr. Moorinski. He was a regular substitute teacher for Cherry Run, and the same fat-assed guy who stood in for Bug Eyes way back in seventh grade and got me my stupid nickname. Carl was raring to go. He had six hundred points to Pooch's nine hundred. Pooch felt safe and smug. Three hundred points would take forever on regular dares.

"Gimme one," Carl whispered during the morning announcements.

I missed this game so bad I didn't even have to think. "When Moorinski calls your name for attendance, you have to dance and sing that you're here."

"Shit. Gimme a different one."

"Nope. Take it or leave it."

"Shit. How many?"

"Thirty."

"You're crazy."

"Come on, thirty points, man. Just like that."

"Make it fifty."

"Bullshit."

"I'll make it worth fifty. I'll make it big."

Moorinski pointed a chubby finger at us. "Zip the lips over there."

I looked at Pooch. He was cool as a cucumber. Not worried at all. I whispered to Carl, "You'll get between thirty and fifty depending on how good it is."

Moorinski was well into the attendance roll. "Graff?" he said.

"Here."

"Hines," Moorinski said.

"Here."

"Kaplan," Moorinski said.

Carl jumped out of his seat, started twisting from side to side and sang, "I'm here, I'm here, I'm really, really here!" His little body jerked across the room. Everyone was staring and Moorinski's mouth was in the shape of a Cheerio. Pooch and I were losing it. Then Carl did a lop-sided cartwheel and landed smack on his ass. All tomato-faced, he came back to his seat looking like he couldn't believe it either. Moorinski didn't know what to say. He just shook his head in amazement. Pooch and me were busting and trying to hold it because everyone else was just staring. One of the Jocks in the back of the room said, "What an asshole."

"That's fifty," he whispered to me. A drop of sweat rolled past his ear.

I looked at Pooch. His long legs were all stretched out in front of him. It was like he was already king. He was sitting back enjoying the view as Carl made an ass out of himself. "A definite fifty," I whispered to Carl. "That was great," I added, because I knew the comment from the Jock was bugging him.

"Gimme another one."

"Are you serious?"

"Do it."

I was off guard. I couldn't believe he wanted another one so soon. I looked around the class. Some people were still looking over at us. I saw the pencil sharpener on the opposite side of the room. "Skip to the pencil sharpener."

"How many?"

"Twenty-five."

"Just skip over?"

"And back."

"Make it thirty."

I thought for a second. "Skip over *and* back for thirty, but if you chicken out halfway, you get nothing."

Carl took a breath, and snapped the point off of his pencil. Moorinski was still droning out the attendance. "Springer?"

"Here."

Then Carl, plain as day, skipped up the aisle, across the front of the room, and over to the pencil sharpener, his shiny black hair bouncing all over the place.

Moorinski stopped calling roll and watched him. One of the Jocks, I think it was Rodney Foreman, said, "What the hell's his problem?"

Me and Pooch were loving it. Old Carl was sharpening his pencil as serious as a judge. Then Moorinski said, "Steven?"

Stevie Myers said from the back of the room, "I'm Steven, he's Carl."

Carl kept sharpening. Moorinski said, "Carl?"

"Huh?" Carl looked over his shoulder.

"What are you doing?"

"Sharpening my pencil."

"Do you always skip across the room?"

"No."

"Then why are you doing it today?"

"Because I'm happy," Carl said, and I lost it.

"That's nice, Carl. But do you mind controlling your happiness until homeroom is over?"

Carl shrugged and looked at me. I wasn't budging. The deal was skip over *and* back or no points. Carl took forever on that sharpening job and finally Moorinski went back to attendance. "Stockman?"

"Here."

And Carl skipped back.

Foreman said, "What is he, a faggot?"

Moorinski swallowed hard and said, "You're trying my patience, mister." After a long minute, he went back to attendance.

"Six hundred and eighty," Carl whispered. "I want a hundred-point dare."

I'd never seen Carl like that. He was unafraid, burning out of control. A hundred-point dare? After everything he'd just done? I couldn't even think of anything.

"Come on, man."

Pooch was looking a little concerned and I liked that. I looked around. Moorinski was staring at Carl every few seconds. His plump face was getting red and veiny. The nimrod didn't seem to know I was in on it, so I looked innocent as hell when he looked over. When I couldn't help laughing, I would look at Carl and shake my head like I couldn't believe what a weirdo he was. When Moorinski looked away, I whispered, "Call Moorinski, Fat Ass."

"A hundred points?"

"That's all I got for Monkey Face *and* three swats!" Pooch said.

"This is different," I said. "Moorinski is already pissed off. It's more dangerous."

"A hundred points?" Carl still wanted to know.

I couldn't believe he was considering it. No argument.

"Yeah," I said. "A hundred points."

"No way," Pooch said, but we both ignored him. "Give me one."

Carl stared at Moorinski. I was on the edge of my seat. My heart was pounding away. I didn't know what the hell was going to happen next. "I can't do that one," Carl said. "Not now. Gimme another one."

I didn't argue. He was hot. I knew I could get just about anything out of him, and he wanted big ones. Hundred pointers. We were standing to do the Pledge of Allegiance and it hit me. "Say the Pledge of Allegiance extra loud," I said, then added, "and say it in a funny voice. For a hundred points."

"I pledge allegiance to the flag," we all said in unison and nothing was out of the ordinary. "Of the United States of America." Still nothing. I thought Carl had dropped it when he hit, "And to the Republic—" with a screechy voice that sounded something like Jerry Lewis in the old movies and Edith Bunker singing the theme song to *All in the Family.*

Everyone looked away from the flag. Hands over hearts, still half mumbling the words, they stared at Carl. He went on like Edith Bunker on drugs.

"No more!" Moorinski shouted and charged toward Carl. "Get out of here. Now! Get out of my classroom."

Carl was out of his freaking mind. Moorinski grabbed his shirt and pulled him toward the front of the room. Carl sounded like there were tears in his voice and he said, "Let go of me, FAT ASS!"

"Fuck!" Pooch half whispered. "That shaky little fucker just got two hundred points."

No one could believe what was going on. Pooch was muttering behind me, "He's got eight hundred and eighty fucking points. Give me one."

I couldn't. I was stunned. I couldn't believe what the hell was happening. Everyone was amazed. Moorinski was throwing a fit, and fucking Pooch wanted a dare!

"A hundred pointer," he hissed at me. "Now!"

"You're nuts!" I said.

"What if I throw a penny at Moorinski?"

"Huh?"

"A hundred points for nailing him with a penny?"

I couldn't think. Moorinski threw Carl out of the room and slammed the door.

"A hundred points?" He was on my back.

"Ah...okay!"

"All I have is a nickel," he said and the next thing I knew it bounced off of Moorinski's ear.

Moorinski let out a girlie, "Ow!" and his hand covered his ear. Then, he spun around on his Hush Puppies and was flying right toward us like there was no tomorrow. Old Fat Ass was serious as hell but Pooch was laughing at him.

I felt bad for Moorinski for a minute. He didn't know what the hell to do. His forehead had this giant vein sticking out that looked like the letter Y. He yanked Pooch out of the chair and slapped him on the head when he resisted.

That sobered Pooch up fast and he threw Moorinski off of him. I'd forgotten how strong old Pooch was.

"Get out of here!" Moorinski said. "Go to the office."

"I'm going," Pooch said. "Just leave your hands off of me." And out the door he went.

Moorinski stood there for a minute. Like he was lost in a snowstorm. And then he went out the door too.

The whole class started mumbling then as if closing the door turned on a talk switch. My heart was still racing. Wow! Old Carl. Man. And Pooch too. Both at the office. We were going to have to lay low for a month after that one.

"Hey Jack-Off, your ass is grass," Foreman said.

"What?"

"You're fucked big time."

"I didn't do anything."

"Like hell. I saw you telling them what to do."

"We all did," Cohen said.

"Bullshit."

Cohen jumped out of his seat. "Are you calling me a liar?"

I hated these assholes. I wished they were dead.

"I think he's calling all of us liars," Foreman said.

"I'm talking to you, Jack-Off."

I just stared straight ahead. Those assholes were next on the list. And it would be worse than fox piss. I could feel Cohen staring at me. He started up the aisle towards me with the whole damn room watching.

Moorinski walked in. "What's going on here?"

"Nothing," Cohen said.

"Get back in your seat. The bell for the first class is about to ring." He went back to the teacher's desk and Cohen retreated.

"We have gym class today, Jack-Off," Foreman whispered up at me.

"We're going to tell Henderson we all want to play Shake, Rattle, and Roll," Cohen said.

"Keep it down," Moorinski said, "unless you want to join those two jokers in the office."

I kept staring straight ahead. Shake, Rattle, and Roll made Dodge Ball look like hopscotch. It was a game Henderson made up. It looked like full contact soccer, but was really just an expanded version of Smear the Queer (the queer being anyone the Jocks didn't like).

The Jocks always had a few guys they wanted to get and if the ball came anywhere near those guys, regardless of what team the guys were on, they had every right to slam, tackle, kick, and punch them. Henderson got a charge out of watching his Jocks kick ass. As long as no fistfights broke out and no blood was spilled, he wouldn't stop the play.

Before first period was half over, a couple of the Brains from homeroom were called to the office. Old Bernie knew they were all goody-two-shoes and would spill everything they knew. About fifteen minutes later a bunch of homeroom Jocks were called. I knew I was screwed then.

It had suddenly hit me that Pooch was the new king. The flying nickel crowned him.

I no more than sat down in second period when I heard my name called over the intercom. I was shaking a little inside when I walked down the empty halls. The Jocks came out of the office and walked toward me.

"You can kiss your ass good-bye," Cohen said.

Foreman smacked his hands together. "Try to make it back for gym."

Mrs. Miller looked down her pointy face at me when I walked in. "They're waiting," she said, and pointed to Bernie's door on the other side of the detention room.

I walked in. Pooch and Carl were sitting in the two big vinyl visitors chairs. Bernie was pacing around the room carrying the paddle. "The Communicator" was painted across it in black letters and there were holes drilled in it so it would whistle when he swung it.

"Shut the door," Bernie said, and I did it quietly.

I looked at Pooch and Carl, but they both stared at the floor. It felt weird. I wanted to catch their eyes just for a second so we'd all know that when it was over we could crack up about how scared we were. But they weren't looking. Carl might have even been crying but I wasn't sure.

"Should we bow?" Bernie said. "I mean the king has graced us with his presence."

They told. Pooch and Carl had told. I looked at them and they just stared at the floor.

Bernie gestured at his chair with the paddle. "Here, take my chair."

I just stood there. I didn't know what to do.

"Come on, king. Take the throne." Pooch and Carl still weren't looking. Bernie growled, "Sit down!"

I walked in front of him half expecting him to slam me with the board. The damn chair practically swallowed me. I sat there and saw a picture of him, his wife, and his three daughters. All smiles and dressed up. I had a flash of him humping Mrs. Miller.

"Your little game is going to cost your loyal subjects here three swats apiece. What do you think of that?"

Pooch and Carl both looked at Bernie like it was news to them. Bernie was actually waiting for me to answer.

"I asked you what you thought of that."

"I don't like it," I said.

"Really? I would think you might find that rather amusing."

"I don't."

He looked at Pooch and Carl. "I'd like nothing more than for the king here to stand up there and take swats with you, but his father paid me a visit a while back to tell me I didn't have permission to do that."

Pooch looked at me.

"I'll take the writing assignment instead," Carl said. His eyes were watery and he was visibly trembling.

"I am not offering you a choice."

"My parents don't allow it either," Carl said.

That was bullshit and Bernie knew it. Carl's old man flew the coop long ago, and his mom was a tramp who spent more time hanging out at the bars than she did at home.

Pooch looked over at Carl like he was disgusted with him. If Pooch was scared, you couldn't tell it.

Bernie said, "I think you should come along and see what your little game is going to cost your so-called friends."

I hated him. The four of us went out to the hallway and he called Mrs. Miller to come along as an adult witness. It was horrible, and it was even worse with old Pointy Face there. She had her arms crossed and was half smiling.

Carl started to bawl. "Please, Mr. Kavanaugh," he said. I wished he would have just shut the hell up! He made everything worse, and there was no way Bernie was going to let him off anyway. The dumb ass even said that he had a medical condition.

I knew it was the end of everything. The game was gone forever, and so were our friendships. At least the kind of friends we were when we played the King Game. I mean, I could tell Pooch was mad I wasn't taking swats with them and I was embarrassed for Carl. We'd never be able to think of him as a regular guy again.

One time, Pooch looked at him and laughed. The meanest damn laugh I ever heard.

Carl only half bent over, like he was going to run for the door any minute. Bernie said, "Stand perfectly still. If you flinch, you'll get an extra one." He walked a good five or six steps, turned around and aimed the paddle like he was at the starting line of some new sport. Then he ran and swung the board at the same time. His jacket flew behind him like a cape, and he slammed the paddle into Carl's bony ass, lifting him right off the ground. Carl screamed and stood up, grabbing his rear end. That seemed to scare Bernie like maybe the kid did have a medical condition or something, so he told him to go to his next class. When Carl started to go, Bernie said, "Don't you want to thank your good friend here, the king?"

Carl just kept going. Bernie looked at Pooch and said, "Show him how to take it like a man."

Pooch assumed the position and Bernie walked his usual steps up the hall and came running back, smacking the board against Pooch. The paddle whistled and cracked each time. Bernie was really swinging that thing. He was breathing heavy after three. But Pooch just stood up and said, "Can I go now?"

"I don't know. Can you?" Bernie said.

Pooch made a face. "May I?"

"Yes, you may."

Pooch looked at me.

He shook his head.

He walked away and I felt like nothing.

It's 2:50.

Five more minutes. I made it through another day.

Detention sounds like a big deal, but Pooch and Carl don't care. They think I got the easy way out, and I suppose I did.

So it's just me again. Alone. Me and my thoughts.

I turn over my tablet to do my favorite task of the day: marking off the countdown sheet.

Two days of detention left.

152 days of ninth grade left.

692 days of Cherry Run High School left.

Without the King Game, it's really going to crawl.

FREE BIRD

Thanksgiving was next Thursday, and if Clayton could stand the job that long, he'd get a free turkey. A week and a half was a hell of a long time for a guy hooking pork bellies with nothing more than a free bird to look forward to. It was a stupid job. And it was no better than any other job he'd had. His girlfriend, Nancy, thought this one might be different, but if you asked Clayton, that was just wishful thinking. His jobs were always the same. The boss was a jerk, and most of the guys were assholes. Just the thought of the place gave him a headache. He'd had enough of being cold every day and looking at the ugly bloodstains on the floor. It felt like he had been there for years, and it had only been two months. Two months of this stuff was enough. More than enough.

The problem was that he'd already told Nancy about the turkey. She was pretty excited about it. Nan hadn't been excited about anything for a long time, so he could hardly quit early. She had plans for that turkey. "Let's have a real Thanksgiving feast," she said. Clayton didn't know where she got off using the word "feast." Then she went on about how when she was a little girl, before her old lady took off, they'd go to her grandparents' house for Thanksgiving. She'd chatter on and on about all these different kinds of food and how her grandma would let her baste the turkey.

Clayton really didn't know about this Thanksgiving stuff. It seemed like the kind of thing other people did. He never had a regular Thanksgiving. Maybe once or twice, but he didn't remember it. His old man probably got tanked and ruined the whole deal, no doubt. Besides, what the hell did he have to be thankful for? A lousy job? A junk car? An apartment that was drafty as hell?

But it was too late to turn back now. Nancy was making a list. Potatoes and noodles. A loaf of white bread, an onion, and celery for the stuffing. Pie filling, a ready-made crust, and carrots. "Who likes carrots?" he said to her when he read the list. "I don't."

"They won't be regular carrots when I'm done fixing them," Nan said. "They'll be glazed. Grandma used to make them. They were sweet and kind of mushy." That reminded her that they would need more sugar and butter. This free bird was costing Clayton a pile of money.

Nancy was figuring how to make everything. She said she wished she could call her grandma and ask her how she did it. Then she got all sad for a while, thinking about how the old woman was dead and buried ages ago, and how her grandma's house was either torn down or being lived in by other people. She didn't know which was worse.

Clayton couldn't stop her sadness. Not once she got started. She'd talk about her mom running off and leaving her. He didn't know what the point was in feeling bad about things. Life is a bitch. That's just the way it is. Hell, she had it better than he did. He wished his old man and old lady would have run off and left him alone instead of hanging around and fighting and knocking the crap out of him and his brother. He tried telling her stuff like that before, that life was just that way, and crying about it or wishing it were better just made things worse. Nancy was too damned soft. He was glad he wasn't like that, at least.

She straightened up by the time she had to go shopping for the stuff. He was glad for it. He didn't even say anything about her forgetting to buy his lottery ticket or the grocery bill being way too much. Onto the list she had to add a special pan for the turkey. It was made of thick foil, so it was cheap enough. A baster had to be bought too. It looked like a giant eyedropper. He couldn't find a price on it. She said they were things that they needed. But then she turned around and bought candles and these little candle holders that looked like pilgrims with holes in their heads. Clayton sure hoped he was up to all of this.

Two days before Thanksgiving, some man in a refrigerated truck handed each guy a turkey on their way out of the building. The super was standing with the turkey man and was all smiles with his clipboard. He marked off each guy who got one and said, "Happy Thanksgiving." The first two words the guy ever said to Clayton. Probably the last. Clayton decided to stay with the job a while longer. Probably not much, but a few days. They had the whole weekend off, anyway. When he handed the turkey to Nancy, she took it and kissed him on the cheek. She said it was a good-sized one and that they'd have lots of leftovers. When she was a kid, leftovers were a big deal. "Sometimes it even tastes better cold," she said.

She found a little booklet inside the wrapping telling her how to fix the bird. It had to thaw in the refrigerator for two days.

On the big day, she had him up at 7:00 in the morning. What the hell kind of day off was that, he wanted to know. She asked him to please not swear on Thanksgiving day.

She was melting butter and chopping up onions and celery for the stuffing and had him pulling things out of the turkey: the neck and a plastic bag with the heart and liver in it. Digging around in the turkey didn't make him too excited about eating it. She washed the bird carefully and then filled every hole full of stuffing and set it in the oven. She was the big boss of the operation. She had him peeling potatoes. She dug up the radio and turned on some weird station that played piano music. She called him to the oven when it was time to pour melted butter over the turkey. Basting, she called it.

They filled the big eyedropper with butter and squeezed it all over the turkey. It was a light shade of brown already and looked good enough to be on a TV commercial or a cooking show. It smelled great. The whole place smelled great. When the turkey was basted and the potatoes and noodles were ready to be put on the stove, Nancy went upstairs.

She put on make-up and fixed her hair.

"Where are you going?" Clayton asked.

"Nowhere," Nancy said.

"What are you getting all dolled-up for?"

"For you," she said, smiling at him like she did when they first met.

Clay felt a little stupid in his underwear and decided to get in on it. He put on a good pair of jeans and a nice shirt that he only wore once before, to his brother's wedding. Nan put on a dress, and she looked sharp. Real good. The kind of woman that a guy would whistle at if she walked down the street.

And she was his girl. He and his girl were sitting on the couch in their own place watching a parade on TV.

"Maybe someday we'll go there and see the parade for real," he said.

"This is real," she said and kissed the side of his nose. Her breath smelled like Wrigley's spearmint gum.

"I mean New York City."

"That might be nice. But I'm glad we're not there now. All those people crowding around. I'm glad we're here in our little place together, having a big feast. I'm thankful for that."

Clayton's stomach tickled. He shifted on the couch and thought he might say something nice to her, but his face got warm and he felt so strange all of a sudden, almost teary-eyed. He focused on the parade, a giant sled pulling a waving Santa Claus, until the weird feeling passed. Then it was time to baste the turkey some more and put the rest of the food on the stove.

She told him all about her grandma's house again, and she said the smell of the warm kitchen and all of the food was just like it was then. Clayton turned out to be pretty darned good at making mashed potatoes. Nancy said so, but even before that, he was thinking he was a natural. Things went real smooth except for a few hectic minutes when everything was getting done at the same time.

The food looked perfect, like a picture on the front of some women's magazine. Nancy covered the card table with a clean, blue bed sheet. She put all of the food on the table and took a picture. Then she took one of Clayton sitting with the food and had him take one of her with the food.

"Maybe we should go next door and have someone take a picture of us together," Nancy said.

Clayton was hungry as a bear. His mouth was watering. He almost got mad at her, but then he took the camera, stood next to her, and with arms outstretched, snapped a picture of them.

"We won't be able to see the food," she said.

"We'll know it's there," he told her and was glad that she didn't argue.

The table bowed in the middle and Nancy suggested that they move the turkey into the kitchen to carve it. "You carve it," she said.

"I don't know how. This is your show."

"It's our show. Besides, it's a tradition."

"There's no tradition here. I've never done anything like this before."

"It will be a tradition," she said. "We'll start it."

Clay liked the idea of starting a tradition. The knife was not very sharp, and he thought that maybe next year he'd buy a fancy one just for the occasion. The turkey was golden brown and juicy. As he sliced up the turkey, she took everything off the table and set it in the kitchen where they could serve themselves. By the time he sat down, she had the candles lit and had poured grape juice into two fancy glasses that he'd never seen before.

"Where'd those come from?"

"A surprise. I got them on sale. They'll be part of our tradition."

Clay was just about to dig in when Nancy said, "We have to pray."

"Pray?"

"Yeah. Give thanks to God."

Clay looked at her like maybe she was kidding.

She wasn't. "My grandma did. The pilgrims did, too."

Clay looked at the candle holders and imagined them praying. "Well, go ahead."

"I thought maybe we could do it together."

Clay had never said a prayer before and didn't think he wanted to start now. "Why don't you do it?"

"I'd like us to do it together."

Clay looked at the floor. "I don't know how."

"I don't either. Not really."

"Then maybe we shouldn't."

"I think we should."

Clay thought the food would be cold if they didn't get on with it. Nancy took his hand and bowed her head. Clay bowed his head. He saw her eyes were shut. He closed his. They sat there for a few seconds and Clay thought maybe she was praying silently when she said, "Dear God, thank you for this food. Thank you for this day. For giving us good health and letting us find each other in this big old world." She stopped and squeezed his hand. She whispered, "Do you want to add anything?"

He didn't think he did. Then he blurted out, "Thanks for Nancy and the turkey and all the other stuff." He felt the weird tingling in his face again like he was going to get all weepy. It felt good and bad at the same time. He didn't want to cry here at the table with Nancy next to him. He never cried. Ever. And he was sure he didn't want to start now, so he thought about how he made the mashed potatoes: mash, milk, mash, butter, mash, mash. And the teary feeling went away. Nancy squeezed his hand and said "Amen."

They opened their eyes and tears were running down Nancy's face.

"What's the matter?"

"Nothing," she said. "I'm happy. I feel good. This is really nice."

"It is. Let's eat."

And they did. They ate and ate and finished off the grape juice. Then they went back to the couch. Clay went to turn on the TV. "Wait," Nancy said. "How about we don't turn the TV on? Why don't we just talk?"

"What do you want to talk about?"

"I don't know. Our tradition. Or anything."

They laid in each other's arms, and Clay tried to think of what to say until he fell asleep.

When Clayton woke up, it was dark outside and Nancy was staring at him. She said, "Do you think I could be a good mom?"

"Yeah. I guess. Sure."

"If we ever have kids, we can never leave them." Nan was looking all sad again. "Kids don't understand stuff like that."

"There's no reason to be sad," Clay said as he moved toward the leftover turkey and helped himself. Nan was right about the the bird tasting even better cold. "You'd never leave our kids."

"How do you know? What if it's in my blood? What if I'm like her?"

"You're not."

"How do you know?"

"'Cause I know. I know you. You won't do that. You learned from your old lady's mistake." Clay was about to go for another piece of turkey when he noticed Nancy was staring at him like he was saying the most important thing. "I know I learned from my old man. I'd never hit my little kid. Even if he was a brat, I wouldn't hit him."

"What if you got so mad that you couldn't stand it?"

"Then I'd hit a tree or something."

Nancy laughed.

"What?"

"I just imagined you hitting a tree."

"Hey, I mean it," Clay said. "I'd pound the hell out of an old tree before I'd lay a hand on my own kid."

"Wouldn't it be nice," Nan said, "if we could have kids that would never get hit and never get left behind?"

"We can," Clay said. "We could make it part of our tradition."

Nancy went to him in the dim light and touched his face. "You and me. We could, couldn't we?"

"Darn right," Clayton said. "I'd bet on it. I'd bet everything I have on it."

THE KIDS

Earl Hardy crawled out of his warm bed. It was still dark outside. Another day already. His head was pounding and his back was angry. The floor groaned under his cracked feet. He lightened his step. Didn't want to wake the kids.

He found the bathroom in the darkness and shut the door before turning on the light. Out of habit, he reached for the faucet, even though nothing would come out of it. Janet had a jug of water next to the sink. That was good. He could at least brush his teeth and splash a little water on his face.

He came out of the bathroom carefully and stopped like he did every morning. He stood in the darkness, closed his eyes and listened to the kids breathing softly in their sleep. It was a warm, comfortable sound. His favorite sound of all. Sometimes it reminded him of when he was one of the kids under the covers and he'd hear his dad going to work in the morning.

He missed the old man a lot. He missed seeing his face, hearing his voice. Missed calling him for advice, asking him how to get out of messes like the one he had with the sink. Or the big one he might soon be facing at the coal mines.

Earl had a bad feeling that the rumors were more than just rumors this time and the layoffs would be for real. Official word would probably come in a week or so. He never thought he'd be so worried about the prospect of not spending five days a week underground with the stink of sweat and sulfur. But all he could think about were the kids.

How would he take care of the kids?

The low rumbling of the coffee maker came from the kitchen where Janet was packing his lunch bucket. He waited until the smell of coffee made its way through the house. Then he waited a moment longer.

The best part of the day, he thought.

Janet was wrapping peanut butter sandwiches in waxed paper when he came into the kitchen. "Peanut butter?" he asked.

"We're out of lunch meat," she said. "I told you the last time you were out to get some."

He sighed.

"What are you going to do about the water?" she asked.

He sat at the table and shrugged his shoulders. Why did he have to know everything? That's what he got for not being rich. People who had money didn't have to know everything. But he did. He had to be a plumber, a mechanic, a carpenter, an electrician, and a TV repairman. It was ridiculous.

He should never have messed with the sink last night. He'd worked in the mines all day and fixed the gas line in the pick-up when he came home. That was enough for one day, but he had to see if he could stop the leak in the kitchen sink, and now he had another mess. He'd worked on it till 2:30 in the morning and it would be waiting for him when he got off work today.

Janet poured him a cup of coffee and sat down across from him with one of her own. She was wearing a blue flannel nightgown that the kids picked out for her last Christmas. It looked comfortable. Her hair was sticking up everywhere and he couldn't help but notice that she was looking older. When did that happen? If she was looking older, he must really be a sight.

"You look terrible," Janet said as if she read his mind.

"Thanks a heap," he said.

"You've got to get to bed earlier tonight."

He took a drink of his coffee and looked at his wife. She was a good gal. He knew he should feel luckier than he did to have her.

"Are you just tired or is there something else bothering you?"

"No. Just tired is all." He sipped his coffee and knew his answer didn't satisfy her. "I don't know," he sighed. "Feeling a little sorry for myself, I suppose."

"Why?"

Earl shrugged.

"You got nothing to be sorry about."

"I know it." He was going to tell her about the layoffs, but decided to wait until word was official. There was no point in both of them worrying all week over rumors.

"It wouldn't hurt to leave a little early," she said. "The roads look pretty slick."

He looked toward the window. It was half frosted over. "You going into town today?"

"The kids have dentist appointments at noon. Remember? I have to take them out of school early."

He sighed. "Don't let that swindler rip you off. If he pulls that x-ray bit, you tell him no. It's not necessary. Every time you turn around, he wants to take x-rays. That's a day's pay right there before he's even touched their teeth." He stood up and his back seized. "Ah shit."

"You need to see a doctor about your back," she said.

"It goes in and out. I don't need to pay a doctor to tell me that," he said, as he straightened up and finished his coffee. "Don't forget to play my number when you're in town." He'd been playing the same number in the state lottery for years now.

"They say there's a better chance of getting struck by lightning," she said, "than hitting that dang thing."

"I believe it." He grabbed his thermos and lunch bucket and stopped at the door for a moment. "You'ns be careful on those roads."

"You too."

"It looks colder than Kelsey's arse out there," he said.

"Below zero."

"Why don't you let the kids sleep in."

"They'd love it, but do you think it's okay?"

"They have to miss half a day anyway. It's a hell of a day to have to go out so early."

"Okay," she said.

"You may as well go back to bed for a while too."

"I think maybe I will."

He put his hand on the doorknob. It was covered with frost.

She said, "Don't worry so much. Everything is fine."

"Yeah," he said, as he pushed open the door.

INITIATION

Seth Hardy got his first real job in the summer of his fifteenth year pruning trees for Rabbleman's Christmas Tree Farm. Rabbleman owned several thousand acres of pine trees in and around Cherry Run and shipped truckloads of them out to cities every December to be sold as Christmas trees. Teenaged boys were always hired to do the pruning because they would accept the pay, which was "under the table" and, therefore, always considerably less than the minimum wage. The job had the reputation of being a last resort for anyone hoping to make some extra money. Those who worked there spent the summer slicing away at the trees in the hot sun and even in the rain, six days a week, all summer long.

Still, Seth was excited at the prospect of having a summer job. He counted up the hours he'd work in a week, twice as many as he would have gotten at Anderson's farm, and figured that if he did a good job of saving, he might have enough to buy a secondhand dirt bike by the middle of August. He could already hear other guys racing around and climbing the spoil piles on the strip cuts behind his house and was eager to get in on the fun.

On his first day, he was to meet the rest of the guys at the Pennzoil station in Cherry Run at 6:30 in the morning. His dad drove him there on his way to the mines.

"I did this same job when I was your age," Earl Hardy said.

Seth knew this, of course, but said, "Did you like it?"

"About as much as I like the mines."

"That much, huh?"

"Same as everything else, it was a job. We had a lot of fun though." He laughed. "We was always raising hell of one kind or another. We did all kinds of shit when old man Rabbleman turned his back. He don't go out with the guys anymore. They got a field boss now. In fact, the guy that will be your field boss was a pruner at the same time I was."

"Really?"

"Hell yeah. Old Heinie Wilkins."

"Heinie?"

"How'd you like to go through life with a handle like that?"

"Why'd they call him that?"

"Who knows."

"Has he always been called that?"

"Long as I remember. Make sure and tell old Heinie who you are. He'll remember your old man. So they got a van to take the guys out in now, huh?"

"I guess so."

"They used to make sure a couple of the guys they hired had cars and then everyone would pile in."

Earl's pick-up pulled into the Pennzoil where a crowd of guys were gathered. "There's your crew," he said.

Seth grabbed his lunch bag and popped the door open.

"Hang on a second," Earl said. He reached under the seat. "Don't forget this." He handed Seth a stainless steel thermos like the one he carried, only this one was brand-new with no dents or chipped paint.

"What?" Seth said.

"If a guy's gonna work, he needs one of these. Your mom filled it up with hot chocolate while you were getting ready."

"Thanks Dad."

"Something hot tastes good in the morning when it's still cool and wet out." Earl took the Ford out of gear and put it back in again. "Better get going," he said.

"Thanks," Seth said again, and slammed the door.

There were fourteen guys waiting for the van. They were standing around with their hands in their pockets, smoking cigarettes, or sitting on their lunch buckets. Most of them were older than Seth and had worked there before. He knew most of them as Heads, the dope smokers of Cherry Run High School.

His first greeting came from Claude Coarsen. "Hey Jack-Off, what the hell are you doing here? You're too squirrely to work out here with the big boys."

Everyone laughed. Seth knew of Coarsen. He was a couple of grades ahead of him. He didn't know that the older guys knew his nickname and he felt sick when he heard Coarsen say it. Not knowing what else to do, Seth smiled and nodded, thinking he would show the older guys that he was easygoing and could take a joke. Of course, it didn't seem to matter what reaction Seth chose. He'd seen the pattern before with the Jocks. It wasn't any different with the Heads. Coarsen wanted someone to pick on, and for whatever reason, he decided it would be Seth. He said,

"You think that's funny, Jack-Off? You won't be laughing after initiation."

"Ooo," Madman said. Madman had long, knotted hair and rotted teeth that he displayed almost proudly when he spoke. "Initiation!"

"Here comes Heinie," someone said, as a rugged blue and white van drove into the parking lot. The guys crowded in and someone shoved Seth as he was about to step inside. He turned around and one of the guys said, "Let's go, get moving."

Seth took the front seat and slid up against the window, but no one sat with him.

Heinie was a wiry, mean-looking guy in his fifties with a wad of Red Man stuffed into one side of his mouth and a rank-smelling pipe clenched in the other.

"Morning," Seth said to him. "I'm Seth Hardy." Heinie looked at him as though he were retarded and then went back to reading the clipboard with all the names of the workers on it.

"Hey Mr. Heinie," one of the big guys in the back said, "you ain't hung over, are you?"

Heinie looked up from the clipboard. "You want to walk to the fucking field?" The guys laughed and Seth did too. Then Heinie said, "Where the fuck's Peanut?"

"Damned if I know," was the answer from the back.

Heinie started to pull out. "Well if he can't get his fat ass here on time, then he don't need no fucking job."

The van pulled out, and Seth heard Coarsen say to the guys in the back, "Man, I hope Peanut didn't go to the wrong place to meet us. That would be a shame if someone told him the pick-up point was changed to the Texaco on the other end of town."

Then there was the sound of laughter and palms smacking against each other. Peanut was in Seth's class at school. He was to the Heads what Stevie Myers was to the Jocks: entertainment. His real name, Al Peacon, was transformed into Ass Peanut. Peanut for short. He was grossly overweight with a mass of freckles splattered across his face and one eye that crossed in toward his nose. Seth turned around in his seat to join in with the laughter of the others. When Coarsen noticed, he stopped laughing immediately. "Turn around, Jack-Off." Seth tried to laugh along like before and Coarsen stood up in his seat. He had a very serious look on his face. "I said, turn around."

Seth stopped laughing. He felt his ears burn red. Everyone stared at him. He didn't know what to do. "Why?"

"Because I said."

Heinie shouted, "Sit down."

Coarsen did but added, "Well, tell Jack-Off to leave me alone before he gets hurt."

As Seth turned back around, he said under his breath, "Asshole."

Madman was sitting directly behind him and said, "Ooo, Coarsen! Did you hear that? He called you an asshole."

"He what?"

"Called you an asshole," Madman snickered.

"You're gonna pay for that, Jack-Off. You are gonna pay, boy," Coarsen said.

Seth felt the uneasiness in his stomach rise and fall. Coarsen made sure that he heard what was being said about him. "Look at him up there," Coarsen said. "Did you see him staring back here at us? He must be a faggot. He probably wants to suck us all off." He shouted, "Forget it, Jack-Off, you ain't sucking my dick."

Seth wondered why things were the way they were. He was once again reminded how sick he was of this town and so many of the assholes in it. It was a damn shame, he thought, that there had to be people like Coarsen. He was screwed now, this job was screwed, he was already labeled and there wasn't a damn thing he could do about it. He looked at the shiny thermos in his hands and felt sorry for his dad. He was sure his dad didn't know what the guys thought of his son.

Three more years, Seth thought, three more school years until graduation and this piss-ant town will be a memory. It didn't matter where he would go, just as long as it was away from here.

Before they were ten minutes out of town, half of the guys were smoking cigarettes. The air was blue with smoke. Seth felt his stomach turn. All of the windows were up. Seth thought of opening one, but knew it would only draw attention that he didn't want. It would give them one more reason to pick a fight with him. So he scrunched down in his seat and pulled his shirt up over his nose. He wanted them to forget that he was even there.

It took about twenty-five minutes to reach the tree patch. The pine trees went as far as anyone could see. They were only a few feet apart and were planted in rows. Everyone bailed out and Heinie handed machetes to each guy from an old wooden box that lay across the passenger seat. He took the last one and told Seth to follow him over to a tree. "You see this?" he pointed to the light green end of a pine tree branch. "That's new growth. When you're trimming, you want to cut off about half of that. You want to hit the tree at an angle so it's cone-shaped, and when that's done all the way around you find the leader at the top."

The leader was the point on top of the tree. "If there ain't one, make one." He chopped away the top pieces of the tree and left a tall one standing in the middle. It was where some family would put the star or the angel when the tree was cut down and dragged into their home for Christmas.

Heinie handed Seth the big knife. "Do one."

Seth hit the tree and jumped back when cold, morning dew sprayed all over him.

"It's just water," he said. "You'll be soaked in the first ten minutes and it will dry by afternoon, so don't go trying to avoid it. Go on, get to it."

Seth worked his way around, swinging hard, wanting to impress Heinie because he knew his dad. It would be nice to have someone on his side. Maybe it would make a difference. One time the knife deflected off the tree and stuck into the ground with a thud.

"Watch what the fuck you're doing," Heinie said. "Now look where that blade is at in relation to your foot." It was about two inches from the toe of Seth's boot. "We had some dumb fuck slice off two of his toes a couple of summers ago. Not only that, but slamming that thing into the ground like that is a sure way to snap the blade in half. These fuckers are expensive, and if you break it you bought it."

Then he pushed between Seth and the tree. "Look at this," he said, pointing to a place on the tree he'd just trimmed. "What'd I just tell you about the new growth? You cut right past it and into the wood!" Little bubbles of sap were bleeding out of the branches. "Not only does it look like shit but it could kill the tree." He gave Seth a serious look and spit on the ground, wiping a string of tobacco juice from his chin with the back of his hand. "You kill enough of them and you'll be out of a fucking job." He handed Seth the knife and said, "Now do it right."

Heinie assigned everyone a row of trees to trim and left a row between each pruner. "You take one down and the other one back," he said to Seth. To everyone else he added, "These are long-assed rows and I want you to be down and back by lunchtime. Let's go. Get to it."

Everyone started hacking at the trees, not talking much. Seth found that Heinie was right about being soaked clear through in ten minutes. To make it worse, there were a lot of high weeds to wade through. Like the trees, they were covered with morning dew. His feet were so wet that he could actually hear the water squirting around between his toes with each step. He was really concentrating on giving the trees a nice cone shape without cutting too deeply, but the effort caused him to fall behind the rest of the guys.

He turned around to see Heinie standing behind him with his hands on his hips. "I'm getting there," Seth smiled.

"You're too fucking slow," he said and walked away.

Seth started to move faster. He swung hard. "Too fucking slow," he thought and slammed the knife hard into the tree. He cut deep. "You want fast, you prick?" he whispered. "I'll give you fast."

He was moving right along when he came to a tree that someone had already trimmed. He looked around, thinking that maybe some of the guys were playing a trick on him. Seeing no one, he moved on. Soon, he found that every other tree he came to was freshly trimmed.

"What the hell?" he said to himself. The other guys were so far ahead of him, he could barely hear them. He trimmed the next tree and sure enough, the one after it was already done.

He stopped cutting and walked around, trying to figure out what was going on. There were trees in every direction towering above him. For a moment he was confused. He wasn't sure which tree was the one he'd done last. Then he knew why every other tree was already done. "Ah shit," he whispered. Somehow, probably when he was trying to trim faster, he'd lost perspective of which way the rows ran. Instead of going down his row of trees, he was going diagonally through the patch. "Damn it," he whispered. "What an idiot."

This would put him even further behind. He still wasn't sure which way was which. He began working his way through the pines, half running, looking in every direction. The wet branches, sticky with sap, slapped against his body, and one knocked him in the face. The smell of the trees was becoming as annoying to him as the constant sloshing of the water in his shoes and the weight of his wet clothes.

He tried to figure out where he was before anyone realized he was lost. Then he heard the van start and drive away. He didn't know what that meant. Backtracking, he could see that he had gone straight for a while, then diagonally. "Come on," he said. "Come on."

He couldn't imagine why the van would be leaving. Then he heard someone running through the patch. He stopped and stood very still. Madman's voice shouted, "Heinie's gone! Heinie's gone! Initiation!"

Immediately, there was the sound of boots rumbling across the ground. And there were yells and hollers. They were running toward him. Seth tightened his grip on his machete and began running in the opposite direction of the footsteps. Between the trees and the weeds, he raced until he came out of the patch.

"Where the hell is he?" someone said from the trees.

Maybe he should let them catch him, he thought. If they called it initiation, then it was probably something everyone had to do. It was probably just some little thing and then it would be over.

Seth turned around just as Madman slammed into him with a full body tackle. The machete flew out of Seth's hands and into the weeds. "I got him," Madman squealed. "I got him!"

Seth struggled. Madman was small, but strong. Seth nearly gagged when he inhaled a dose of Madman's breath. The smell of rotted teeth, tobacco, and pot. The other guys came popping out of the tree patch from different directions, running, laughing, out of breath.

They dived on top of him, pinning his back to the ground. When he was secured, Coarsen crushed his knees into Seth's chest.

"What's the initiation?" Coarsen asked.

"Take his clothes off and throw him on an ant hill," Madman said.

"There's a big one in my row," another voice said. "A couple feet wide at least. Red ants, too. Bite the piss out of him."

"Alright!" someone said.

"Take your machete and chop it up," Coarsen said. "Get them good and pissed off."

The kid ran into the tree patch. Coarsen got off of Seth's chest and he immediately tried to break loose. His arms and legs were forced in all directions and his shirt was pulled up over his head, covering his eyes. Someone undid Seth's jeans. Unable to see, he kicked and struggled frantically. Eventually the jeans were tugged down as a fingernail dug into his thigh, drawing blood. Somehow, he managed to keep his underwear partially on.

"Look at those skinny white legs," Madman howled.

Seth was surprised to hear his own voice screaming and yelling at them. This made them laugh all the more, but he knew they would not laugh, they would not dare laugh if they had any idea how deeply he hated them. No one would laugh if he could get to his machete. No, the laughing would stop on a dime, then.

"He's a feisty little fucker, ain't he?" someone laughed.

"He's a cunt," Coarsen said.

Seth fought hard and nearly the whole crew was in on the game. Seth was dizzy, his shirt still covered his head and his throat felt raw from yelling. Still, he continued to struggle, sure that if he tried hard enough, he could break free.

With guys on each arm and leg, Coarsen instructed them to lift and carry Seth on the count of three. "One, two, THREE!" he shouted and Seth was dragged through the grass and into the weeds of the tree patch. It felt like his arms were coming out of the sockets as they pulled. Then a guy Seth knew as Kurt shouted, "Sideways, let's take him sideways."

Weeds, sticks, and stones scraped the tender skin of his back and sides. His anger burned tears out of his eyes.

"Holy fuck," Coarsen shouted. "Where's this damned ant hill?"

"Down here," the kid hollered from far away.

"Fuck," Coarsen said. "We ain't got time for this shit. Heinie'll be back any fucking minute."

But they continued dragging him until his pants, bunched around his boots, caught onto the tree stump of a previous year's harvest, loosening the grip they had on his legs. Thrashing, Seth managed to break his arms free as well, pulled the shirt off of his face, and rolled to his stomach before the mob piled on top of him again, crushing him into the ground.

"I think he's had enough," Kurt laughed.

"Bullshit," Madman said. "It's got to be worse than that. No way."

"For God's sake, Jack-Off," Coarsen said. "It's nothing to bawl about."

"I think he's been initiated," Kurt said.

"Hell, yeah," another voice said.

"Not yet," Coarsen said, getting on his knees and looking into Seth's face. "You called me something this morning, didn't you?"

"Come on, Coarsen," Kurt said.

"What? It's fucking initiation!"

"Make him say he's a Cherry Run cherry," Madman snickered.

"Okay, you big fucking baby," Coarsen said, "say you're a Cherry Run cherry and you never had any cunt, and we'll let you go."

Seth's mind was racing. He looked right into Coarsen's small, bluish-gray eyes and wanted more than anything to dig his fingers into them and rip them right out of the bastard's head.

"Whoo," a voice said, "never had any cunt, huh, Jack-Off?"

"Shit," Coarsen said. "The closest he's ever been to a cunt was when he was born. Ain't that right, Jack-Off? Say you remember your mommy's cunt. Say it, and you're initiated."

Seth vaulted violently, breaking a leg free and kicking a guy in the face. "Ouch, goddamn it," the guy said and jumped away. "You're going to pay for that, fucker."

"Let's let him go," Kurt said. "He's been initiated."

"He hasn't said a fucking thing," Madman said.

"Say it," Coarsen said, glaring at him. "Say it now. Say you remember your mommy's cunt."

"He's being a tough guy," someone said.

"Just say it and we'll let you go," someone else said.

Coarsen leaned close to his face. There were tobacco

leaves stuck between his teeth and his eyes were mean little slits. "Say it."

Seth rolled his tongue around in his mouth and spit in Coarsen's face. He saw the blue-gray balls twist in their sockets. The next thing he knew, Coarsen was on his feet and slamming his boot into the side of Seth's head.

"Jesus!" someone shouted, and everyone let go of Seth and jumped back.

His ears were ringing and there was a prickling sensation across his face as he got to his hands and knees, but before he could get up, Coarsen kicked him in the chest, knocking the wind out of him.

"You don't spit on me, you son of a bitch!" he screamed.

Seth gagged for air as Coarsen kicked him in the stomach again. He strained for a single breath and Coarsen kicked. "Think you're too fucking good to say it—" and kicked, "think you're too fucking good—" and kicked.

Seth curled into a ball.

Everyone was yelling.

"For Christ's sake, Coarsen, let him go."

"You're gonna kill him."

Kurt pulled Coarsen away.

Someone said, "Heinie's coming," and like magic, everyone was gone. Madman stayed behind a moment longer and said, "You asshole, Hardy. We was just kidding around. You coulda just said it and it woulda been no big deal."

Then it was just Seth.

He lay there, concentrating on breathing and pulling his pants up. Those were the two most important things. There was a little blood in his mouth. It tasted like metal to him.

If Heinie had really come back, Seth saw or heard nothing of him. After a while, he got up. He walked around, spitting, taking in deep breaths. He decided that despite everything, he wasn't hurt too badly. Just sore and scratched.

He thought about leaving. He could quit. Just leave. He was only a couple of miles from Route 68 and from there he could hitch a ride into Cherry Run.

His thermos was still in the van. He couldn't leave without it. And what would he tell his dad anyway? What reason could he give for quitting? His dad never quit. His dad was one of the guys. How would he feel if he knew his own son was pushed out? That his boy gave up and crawled away?

He looked around in the weeds for his machete. When he found it, he went back to the beginning of the patch and from there it was easy to find his original row. Once he started back, it was not hard to see where he had veered off diagonally. He would keep his focus this time by always looking at the last tree he pruned before moving to the next one. It wouldn't be difficult. If these animals could do it, he surely would have no problem.

He took his time and moved at his own pace. He would be fine. The taste of blood lingered in his mouth all morning. He liked it. It made him feel tough. Unafraid of these bastards. If that was the worst they could do, then they'd never be able to hurt him.

In the days ahead, Heinie sometimes bitched him out for being so far behind, but Seth didn't care. The worst he could do was fire him, and that wouldn't be so bad. The other guys left him alone for the most part. Although they would never say it, some of them regretted that things had gotten so out of hand that first day. They quietly respected him for staying on and never saying what he was told to say. At least that's what Seth concluded as the summer wore on.

And Seth had a lot of time to think, plenty of time to draw conclusions, because he was always alone in the group. Coarsen still said things to him here and there, but after the first day they all had Peanut—who made it to the Pennzoil the next day and every day after that—to pick on. Peanut took the brunt of all torture from Coarsen and Madman as though it were just a normal part of life.

Seth did his own thing, which, he realized, was *watching*. Staying alone and watching. After a while, he was sure he could trim faster than anyone there, but he never did. He hung back, letting the group of them move ahead. He smirked at Peanut struggling to keep up with them, trying ignorantly to be one of the guys.

After the first two weeks, Seth was demoted to full-time topper, which meant he was the guy who carried the ladder behind the pack of pruners and trimmed the tops of the trees too high to reach from the ground. The job was usually dreaded because the topper was always alone and weighed down all day with a heavy, wooden ladder.

Seth didn't mind the position at all. It was a good place, he decided, because he could daydream without being bothered. After leaving Cherry Run, he thought maybe he would try to be a writer and see some of the world. One thing he would definitely do is meet girls. Lots of smart, sexy women like his English teacher, Candice Bracknell, whom he sometimes imagined ditching her husband and running off with him.

But life on top of the ladder was good for more than just daydreaming. It gave him the power to watch and listen and still be separate. The perfect place to plan his revenge.

The pruners all but forgot about the lonely topper bringing up the rear while Seth Hardy, watching a lot, listening a lot, and talking very little, grew to know them extensively by mid-summer. He knew that for the most part, the mood of the pack hinged on the whims of two guys: Coarsen (the unspoken leader) and Madman (the unmistakable clown).

He also knew that the pruners were beasts of habit, always hanging together except when one would break off to take a leak or a crap in the weeds or to run back to the van for a drink of water. But no one ever left the pack when Heinie was walking among them, examining the trees.

So with the pruners far ahead and Heinie with them, Seth Hardy slid off of his ladder, scampered back to the van, and for the third day in a row, urinated in Claude Coarsen's brand-new, insulated water jug. Then as a further tribute, he opened Coarsen's lunch and spit in his meatloaf sandwich.

Also, watching over his shoulder, Seth devoured Kurt's apple pie and helped himself to some candy and a slice of watermelon from other randomly selected lunches. Then, just before putting the lunch buckets and water jug back in the exact place he found them, he took a plastic spoon and a can of chocolate pudding from Kurt's lunch and put it in Madman's.

Having his lunch raids done for the day, Seth returned to his ladder and trimmed at full speed until he moved up just behind the group. They were razzing Coarsen about a girl he was going out with.

"Is that the little piece he had at the mall last weekend?" someone asked.

"Little piece is right. She couldn't have been more than thirteen."

"Fucking right," Coarsen said, "I like them tight."

"Sounds to me like you're a baby humper."

Everyone laughed at that one.

"Fuck you," Coarsen said, butchering a tree, something Seth noticed Coarsen always did. "If they're old enough to bleed, they're old enough to breed."

"Really?" Kurt said. "I heard your motto was 'If she's old enough to pee, she's old enough for me.'"

Even Heinie laughed at that and said, without taking the pipe out of his mouth, "Coarsen: cutting too deep, Peanut: not deep enough, and all of you'ns is too fucking slow." Then he left the patch to scope out what area would be done in the afternoon.

Heinie was barely gone when Madman stuck his machete in the ground, and said, "I feel a shit coming on," and left his row.

This was an everyday thing for Madman, and when he returned, Seth watched him pluck off a handful of pinecones. At this time of year they were green, solid, hard weapons, and plentiful in the fields. He lobbed a couple into the tree Coarsen was trimming and bounced one off the ground near his feet.

"Whoever the fuck is throwing pinecones," Coarsen said, "is gonna get their ass kicked."

Madman grinned at Kurt who was standing near him. Kurt barely returned the smile and kept pruning his tree. He was considered the smart one of the group and never had any interest in Madman's little games.

Seth suspected that Kurt's dislike of Madman was heightened by his family's reputation. They were known throughout the area as welfare bums: people who were able, but unwilling to work, and were thereby supported by the taxes of working people.

Seth's dad was disgusted by the "lazy bastards" and Seth felt sure that Kurt's dad, who also worked in the mines, had plenty to say about Madman's family too.

But as with a lot of other things, Madman was oblivious to this. He, like all of the pruners, including Coarsen, liked Kurt. And because Kurt was smart, but not too smart, they all listened when he talked.

Madman took an extra large pinecone and nailed Peanut in the back with it.

"Ouch, damn it," Peanut said, his voice high and frightened.

Madman ducked behind a tree, stifling his laughter. He looked at Kurt and motioned that it was his turn to throw one at Peanut. Kurt shook his head no. Madman urged again. Kurt ignored him. "Why not?" Madman whispered.

Kurt shrugged his shoulders and kept trimming.

The next pinecone stung Peanut on the pale skin of his neck.

"Son of a bitch," he said, slapping his hand to the back of his neck. "Who the fuck?"

Peanut's pain, and especially his anger, were guaranteed to bring laughter from the crew. Several guys imitated him by putting their hands on their necks and exaggerating Peanut's screeching, "Who the fuck?"

That made him angrier. With the machete in his hand, he scanned the mob viciously.

"Don't look at me, you cross-eyed Ass Peanut!" Coarsen said. "You go fucking accusing me and I'll give you something to accuse about."

Peanut turned toward Madman just in time for the next pinecone to strike his upper lip. "Ouch, goddamn it!"

Everyone roared.

"It ain't funny." Peanut sucked his lip. "It's bleeding. It's bleeding, you fucker."

Madman rushed over to Peanut and shoved him to the ground. "You better watch your fucking mouth, asshole."

Heinie yelled, "Lunch!" from the other field and everyone lost interest in everything but running to the van for food. Madman pointed a finger at Peanut, who was still on the ground. "You call me a fucker again and I'll kick your teeth out."

By the time Seth opened his lunch and found some shade to eat in, his private show had begun. Coarsen was drinking from his new water jug. He spit it on the ground. "Fuck," he said. He tasted it again. "Shit." He handed the jug to Kurt. "Taste that, man, it's like it was yesterday."

"No thanks."

"Come on, try it."

"No. I tried it yesterday. It was horrible. I don't want to try it again."

Coarsen screwed off the top, looked inside, and smelled it. "It smells like..." he sniffed again, "asparagus."

Seth, who had asparagus for dinner the night before, was concentrating very hard on not bursting into uncontrollable laughter. He silently commended himself for urinating in the jug only enough to ruin the water, not enough to turn it yellow.

"Where did you get the jug?"

"K-Mart."

"I'd take it back. There's something wrong with it."

"It's been weird every day."

"Take it back."

And several guys were complaining about missing things from their lunch: a piece of pie, candy, watermelon. Seth added to the list in the most defeated but clear voice he could muster, "Someone took my Twinkies."

"If I catch the bastard who keeps taking my pie," Kurt said, "there's going to be hell to pay." Then he looked at Madman eating a can of chocolate pudding with a plastic spoon. "Hey Madman? Where the hell did you get the pudding?"

Madman shrugged his shoulders. "Old lady packs my lunch. Ask her."

"I had one of those puddings this morning with a plastic spoon. Same exact kind as that."

"Well this ain't it. This is mine. My old lady put it in."

Seth concentrated on eating his lunch and minding his own business. This was his favorite part of the day. It's important, he thought, not to overact. Don't look too concerned. Don't look too unconcerned. Just keep it in the middle.

Kurt watched Madman closely, and Seth even noticed him trying to get a look inside Madman's lunch bucket.

"What the hell are you looking at?" Madman asked.

"Nothing," Kurt said. "Just seeing what all you have for lunch."

"I ain't got nothing of yours."

"I didn't say you did. I was just looking."

Coarsen said, "Peanut is probably the thief."

Peanut looked up from his baloney sandwich: one eye aligned, the other askew. "Wasn't me."

"Look at that gut," Coarsen went on. "He could fit everyone's lunch in there and still have room for more."

Peanut's upper lip was swollen where the pinecone struck him earlier. "I was trimming right beside you all day."

"Everybody was," said the guy who lost his watermelon slice.

"Except for Madman," Kurt said.

"Bullshit. I was there."

"You were the only one who left."

"Yeah. I left to take a shit."

"Every day, you have to leave to take a shit."

"I can show you the fucking shit." Madman got to his feet. "Come on, I'll show you the pile."

"I don't want to see your shit."

"Well then don't go trying to say I did something I didn't."

"I never accused you of anything. I just said you were the only one to leave the patch before lunch, and you do it every day."

"Where the hell were you, Hardy?" Coarsen said, chewing a mouthful of meatloaf sandwich.

Seth concentrated on peeling an orange and pretended not to hear.

Coarsen yelled, "Hardy!" Seth jumped and Coarsen burst into laughter and said to the group, "He's like one of them fucking retards that don't know where they're at. What do they call them? Artistic kids or something?"

"What?" Seth asked. "Are you talking to me?"

Coarsen stuffed the rest of the sandwich into his mouth and shook his head. "Nothing, Hardy. Nothing."

That afternoon, Seth decided to trim fast enough to stay only slightly behind the pack in case there were any developments in the case of the lunch thief. At times, he hid behind his tree and burst with quiet, little fits of laughter. He was proud of himself and wished that there were just one person he could tell this to. Someday, he thought, someday. He imagined how he would tell it, imitating Coarsen's face and voice: "It smells like…asparagus."

Madman pouted for a while about being all but accused of stealing Kurt's lunch and probably everyone else's, but he was too high-strung to maintain it. Before long, he was tossing pinecones at various pruners. Kurt was ignoring him completely and a few other guys shouted, "Damn it, Madman!"

"What?" he said with mock innocence.

"Cut it out."

It was always quiet after lunch, and no one got too angry with Madman because he wasn't throwing them hard, except at Peanut, and nobody but Peanut had a problem with that.

Then, standing on his ladder, Seth looked at Coarsen, trimming only a short distance away, and noted that Madman was between the two of them. From the tree, he chose a nice-sized pinecone. He squeezed his fingers around it. It's weight was less than that of a stone and it had a bumpy texture that felt good in his hand. Half hidden by the tree, Seth studied the rest of the pruners. With the exception of Madman, they were all in what Seth thought of as the after-lunch lull. They were doing nothing but trimming the next tree. Barely talking.

Seth gripped the pinecone between his thumb and forefinger. He glanced at everyone again. He looked at Madman, who was quietly plucking more pinecones from his tree. And as hard as he could, so hard that he nearly shook himself off the ladder, Seth Hardy hurled the pinecone with such force that it made a snapping sound when it struck Coarsen in the corner of his left eye.

Coarsen wailed and immediately fell to his knees with both hands covering the left side of his face. Everyone, including Seth, raced toward him. Everyone wanted to know what had happened. Was he okay? What was going on?

Coarsen rocked back and forth saying, "Goddamn, goddamn, son of a bitch, that hurts, son of a bitch!"

"What the hell happened?" Kurt asked.

"Someone threw something at me."

Everyone turned to Madman. He still had three pinecones in his hand.

"You piece of shit," Kurt said.

"It wasn't me," Madman said, "I swear—"

The pinecones were falling from Madman's hand when Coarsen bolted violently into him. For the first few seconds, Madman just tried to keep from getting hurt and to explain to Coarsen that it wasn't him. But Coarsen was a maniac, and after the first clean smack to the face, Madman only wanted to hurt Coarsen as badly as Coarsen was hurting him.

The guys all watched as the two rolled around in the weeds, grunting and growling. Seth looked concerned, but was beaming inside. It was nothing like the fights in the movies with clear, solid punches and fancy moves, but it was better than he could have hoped for. The two were full of hatred, and like every scrap he'd ever been in or witnessed, that kind of hatred resulted in a dirty fight. There was kicking, scratching, hair-pulling, and at one point, after Madman's nose was bloodied, biting.

Once Madman's sharp, blackish-gray teeth broke through the soft skin of Coarsen's cheek, he wouldn't let go. Like a bulldog, he held on, jerking his head from side to side. Everyone was cheering for Coarsen except for Seth. If he had his way, they would fight until one or both of the worthless bastards were dead.

No one even saw Heinie return until he was kicking them apart.

"You fucking assholes," he shouted. He growled at the other guys, "Pull them apart, goddamn it, pull them apart."

Heinie caught Madman by the hair and two other guys grabbed Coarsen's arms. For a few seconds, all five of them were one wriggling mass until Coarsen and the two guys fell one way and Heinie and Madman went the other. There were grunts and yells and accusations. Both were covered in blood and panting wildly.

During the ruckus, Heinie's pipe had been pulled from his mouth so harshly that his upper plate of false teeth were yanked out with it. "Where's my goddamn teeth?" he shouted, and the guys who were standing around began to search.

"Here's your pipe," someone said, and Heinie ripped it out of his hands.

"Your teeth are over here," Kurt said.

"Well give me the damn things."

Kurt looked at them on the ground and said, "I don't want to touch them."

"For fuck's sake, they won't bite, you pansy ass!" Heinie pushed past him and picked them up. He held them up toward the sun and examined them. They were brown from the tobacco and there were little pieces of grass stuck to them. He picked the grass off, wiped them on his pants and shoved them back in his mouth. "Now listen here," Heinie said to the two guys on the ground still trying to catch their breath, "you can be glad my fucking teeth ain't broke or I'd kill both of you. And if I see any more fighting, your ass is out of here. I'll fire you on the spot. And that goes for all you fuckers."

Heinie stood over them while Coarsen and Madman washed the blood off of themselves with the water from Coarsen's water jug and used antiseptic from the first-aid kit. Then they joined everyone else in going back to work.

Since Seth had no one to tell it to, he wrote the whole story in a tablet that he kept under his bed and titled it: "The Day of Reckoning." He also kept track of the rest of the summer at Rabbleman's and decided that someday, if he ever did become a writer, he could put it all in a book.

Coarsen's eye was purplish for weeks from the pinecone and his face would always have a small scar from Madman's teeth. Whenever Seth felt lonely and small, he looked at that scar and felt a little better. And it was comforting to know that on several occasions before and after that day, Coarsen had urine with his water and spit with his sandwiches.

With Coarsen hating Madman and everyone else believing he was a thief, Madman's pranks and games were no longer funny. He became somewhat of a loner himself. So much so that he even tried to make friends with Seth, but Seth wasn't interested either. So a week after the fight, Madman quit the job.

"Preparing to be a reliefer like all the other bums in his family," Kurt said the day Madman didn't show up to work.

By the end of the summer, Seth had saved enough to buy an old Kawasaki dirt bike. He rode it all over the strip cuts after work every evening and all day on Sundays. He was glad he stuck it out at Rabbleman's, but had no intention of returning the next summer, even though he knew they would take him.

And why shouldn't they? A good topper was hard to come by. Especially one that kept his mind on his work and never made any trouble.

PEEPING TIM

Nothing was mentioned. Tim Weaver had listened hard and watched closely over the past two weeks. No strange phone calls. His parents were the same as always. Jodi Case had dropped by to chat with his mother four times since the incident thirteen days ago, and she never said a word about it. He listened intently through the register in his upstairs bedroom during each of the four visits.

Voices drifted cleanly through the ducts of the old house. Lying on the floor with his ear pressed against the register, he could hear every word spoken in the kitchen. His mother and Jodi talked about the usual things: jobs, fashions, kids, husbands, neighbors. But Tim did not hear what he so greatly feared he would.

At first it was a relief, but now it was making him nervous. There was no doubt that Jodi had caught him. It was the fourth time she had forgotten to pull the blinds since the first time last summer. She had stepped out of her clothes, tossing some in the hamper and hanging others in the closet, just as she had the times before. But that night, instead of crossing her bedroom and stepping into the bathroom, she turned and looked out of her window across the strip of lawn and right into Tim's bedroom window. Her mouth dropped open and her arms went to her naked breasts, squashing them as she covered herself. The binoculars fell out of Tim's hands and hit the floor at about the same time he did. His heart was pounding in his ears. Finally, when he got the nerve to peek out of the window, her blinds were down.

They had remained that way ever since.

It was his own fault, he reasoned. The night wasn't dark enough. He was careless, stood too close to the window. It had been so perfect. Just moving next door to a woman who looked like Jodi was a miracle, but seeing her peel off a pair of shorts or jeans and unhook her bra and let it slide down her arms was incredible. Without even knowing it, she gave herself to him. Every turn of her head or toss of her hair, every scratch or rub, every movement was for his private pleasure.

Having Jodi next door was better than a subscription to *Playboy*. Along with knowing her nakedness, Tim got to know her voice, her laugh, her life, as they echoed through the register. Though her presence made him too anxious to talk to her on these visits, he often staged a good entrance to grab a snack, and then casually exited back to his bedroom where he could hear everything uncensored.

Today marked Jodi's fifth visit, and still nothing was said. Some days it overwhelmed Tim that no matter where Jodi was or what she was doing, she was always naked beneath her clothes. It tickled him that he didn't have to imagine her nudity; he simply had to remember. Even now, as she complained with his mother about the high cost of living, her breasts were quietly resting under her shirt with their wide, pink circles of nipple. She had once told his mother that they were a full cup size larger since the baby. Tim imagined them growing overnight while she slept. And then there was her ass. It had a slight jiggle to it when she walked across her bedroom naked.

It was enough to drive a guy insane.

"Hair is a sensuous thing," he heard Jodi say. The word "sensuous" jumped out at him. She was discussing the expense of having her hair highlighted every three months. Tim thought of her hair hanging over her shoulders. "John loves it," she said. "He's been sold on it since the first time I surprised him with it."

John was her husband. Tim couldn't imagine how a normal-looking guy, who even had a balding head, could have ended up with a woman who looked like Jodi. He had never seen them having sex, but he did imagine it a couple of times. Apparently they never did it with the blinds open.

Jodi's mention of hair got his mother going. She whined about the financial strain of having eleven and thirteen-year-old kids. He hated it when she referred to him as a kid. His eleven-year-old sister was a kid. He was not.

"Timmy grows out of things as quick as I buy them," his mother said. "And I can't believe what they charge to cut his hair down at the Shear Shack."

Jodi wasn't surprised. She told his mother that she used to cut hair. In fact, to save money, she still cut her husband's hair, and occasionally the hair of a young nephew. "If you want," Jodi said, "I'd be willing to cut Tim's hair to help you out."

Tim's whole body tightened.

"Oh, I couldn't ask you to do that," his mother said.

"Don't be silly. You help me all the time. I'd love to do it."

Tim wasn't breathing.

"But you're so busy."

"It'll take a half hour at the most," Jodi said. "We'll just keep it quiet so I don't end up doing the whole neighborhood."

"That would be such a help," she said. "Of course, I don't know if I can get him to do it. He is so particular about his hair. We've tried to get him to go to cheaper places, but he always raises such a ruckus."

"Really?" Jodi said. "He seems like such a quiet boy."

"You just don't know him," his mother snorted. "But he has been going through a weird stage lately. Very to himself, always reading comic books or watching movies in his bedroom. Better than a lot of other things he could be doing at this age, though." Then she shouted, "Timmy!"

His heart was thumping against the floor. Movement came back to him with a jolt. He found himself standing in the middle of his room.

"Tim!" she called a second time.

He took a deep breath, and trying to sound disinterested, he answered, "What?"

"Could you come down here for a minute?"

Tim swallowed and whispered, "Holy shit." This made no sense to him. Jodi knew there were things he did in his bedroom that had nothing to do with movies and comic books. He knew she knew, even if she hadn't said so. He took another breath. And now she wanted to cut his hair? If she cut his hair, she would be touching him. He cleared his throat, and when he felt his mother was going to shout a third time, he went downstairs.

Jodi sat in the chair that he always sat in when the family ate supper. Her legs were neatly folded under her. She wore a white tee shirt, a faded pair of jeans, and scuffed-up sneakers. She looked at him; it felt like a pinch. It was not a happy look at all. He was sure that she was about to spill the beans to his mother.

But Jodi said nothing. His mother explained the situation and reminded him that he was due for a haircut. She pointed out how nice it was of Jodi to offer, and that she had a lot of experience cutting hair. At some point Jodi told him, "You don't have to decide right now. Think about it and let me know." Then she added, "It would give us a chance to get to know each other a little better. You're so quiet."

Somewhere in there he had said that it would be okay with him. That he was sick of the Shear Shack anyway. And they had decided to do it the next day right after he got home from school. She didn't work Thursdays, her husband wouldn't be home until much later, and the baby would be down for a nap. As he went back upstairs in a kind of stupor, he heard his mother comment on how easy it was to get him to agree. Jodi's words, "a chance to get to know each other" and "John won't be home" and "the baby will be napping," quivered through his brain.

Sleep was impossible that night. Tim played the scene over and over in his mind. It seemed too good to be true, but she did make a point of saying that it would only be the two of them, and that they could get to know each other better. She did say that. It was not his imagination. And she never said a word about catching him.

He remembered a story he once read in his cousin's *Penthouse* about a woman who lured the pizza delivery boy into her bedroom and screwed him all evening. Tim redirected the story in his mind with Jodi and himself in the leading roles. He promised himself that this would be the last time tonight because he was getting sore down there. Besides, he had to save himself for tomorrow, in case Jodi really did mean what he hoped she meant by "getting to know each other."

School was painfully slow. He wore a long shirt to cover the front of his jeans because he knew what kind of day it would be. It was the same shirt he wore now as one shaky hand reached out to knock on the door while the other double-checked his pants pocket for the two rubbers he'd swiped from his parents' dresser drawer. Already, his heart was beating too fast.

"It's open," she called from somewhere inside.

Tim stood in the kitchen, unsure about where to go next. Jodi walked in. She wore a summer dress. Bare feet, bare legs, hair spilling over her shoulders. "Ready for a haircut?" she asked.

He smiled, but no words came out. The top of her dress fit tightly around her breasts. The breasts he knew she knew he saw. He tried to think of something else—the warm weather, the magnets on the refrigerator, the stroller covered with toys— but his mind was all nipples and jiggles. She told him that the only place she had a large enough mirror was in the bedroom. His hands began to sweat. He knew that mirror was attached to her vanity table from his nights with the binoculars.

He followed her upstairs. She pointed to the baby's room and whispered, "She's asleep." He watched her lips as she spoke and wondered what would happen if he just reached out and touched her. When they reached her bedroom, she pushed the door halfway shut and said that the baby was a pretty sound sleeper. Tim wondered if he should be doing any-thing: making a move, saying something sexy. His legs were flimsy. His voice was somewhere in his stomach. So he decided to let her make the first move.

In the bedroom, she had prepared for him. The vanity table with the big mirror had all the perfume bottles pushed to one side. In the center sat a haircutting kit: shiny, chrome scissors and a heavy black pair of clippers. The woman down at the Shear Shack never used clippers. Only scissors, which were dainty with little black handles.

Jodi led him to the chair, which sat on overlapping squares of newspaper. A beach towel was draped over it, and she picked it up for him to sit down. He was thankful that she would cut his hair first. He needed a minute to breathe. To think. Besides, he'd have to go home with a haircut to pull the whole thing off. She pinned the towel around his neck. He took comfort in his familiar reflection as he folded his hands on his lap. There was the smell of her perfume.

"I don't need much of a haircut," he said, finding his voice. "Just a trim."

She didn't say anything. She moved around him with her bare legs and combed his hair in a very slow, careful motion. The hair started to cling to the comb.

Tim cleared his throat. "At the Shear Shack, they wet my hair first."

"Do they?" she said, stepping in front of him, her dress flitting over her legs. "They probably don't use clippers down at the Shear Shack either."

"No," Tim said, sort of suddenly.

Jodi picked up the clippers and moved back behind him. "Well, this will be quite an experience for you." She smiled at him in the mirror. "Relax. I know what I'm doing." Tim let out a breathy laugh. She said, "Could you lean your head forward, please?"

He did. The clippers came on with a small cracking sound. Jodi casually asked him if he liked school, and then buzzed a deliberate course up the back of his head. He lunged forward out of the chair, bumping into the vanity. His hand flew to the back of his head, where he felt a strip of stubble.

"What are you doing?!" he screeched.

Jodi shut off the clippers. "How many times have you spied on me?"

A surge of heat came over Tim. He wanted to say, "never." He wanted to say, "only once." But he just moved his mouth.

"It's up to you. I can tell my husband and your parents about the neighborhood Peeping Tom, which I have not yet done, or you can let me finish the haircut and we'll call it even."

"That's not fair," Tim heard himself say.

"Neither is being watched through binoculars in the privacy of your own bedroom."

He was so overwhelmed, his lip began to quiver.

"Crying doesn't work with me," she said.

"It's not fair," he said again.

"I think it's very fair," she said easily. "Besides, I have no intention of cutting it all off."

He touched the back of his head. "How much?"

"Sit down and I'll show you in the mirror." She laid down the clippers and held open her hands. "I'll just show you."

Tim felt very small. He sat down. Jodi looked at him in the mirror. She gently moved her fingers through his hair. "I cut my five-year-old nephew's hair every summer," Jodi said. "His mother thinks little boys look cute with really short hair. So I clipper off the sides and the back, cut the top really short, and give him some bangs."

Tim shifted in his seat. He noticed he was holding his breath. It seemed he was on the verge of some great emotion, yet somehow in limbo. They stared at each other. Her eyes were stern. He imagined calling her a bitch, but he knew it would only make matters worse. Instead he said, "I'm sorry. I won't do it again."

"I know. My blinds are down now." She picked up the clippers. "Shall we?"

"Mom will hate it," he said, hoping this might save him.

"I never claimed to be a professional. Every time I tried to fix one mistake, I created another. Thank goodness hair grows back."

They looked at each other. The clippers snapped on. Tim took a final look at his hair. Maybe she would take pity on him. "Bend your head forward," she said.

At first he felt claustrophobic. Trapped. Even light-headed. But when it was definitely too late, when there was no going back, it was easier. Jodi was in control. The clippers were a warm vibration on his head. Clumps of hair tickled down his back and tumbled over the white towel. As the cool air touched his neck and ears, Tim surrendered himself to Jodi's smooth, careful hands, so precise in their revenge. He almost relaxed as she moved around him, a breast brushing his shoulder once, her perfume in the air, all of her attention on him as she angled herself this way and that. He wished this part of it could last forever.

She put the clippers down and picked up the scissors. Her legs straddled his and she leaned close to his face. "Shut your eyes," she said. Her breath, smelling like cinnamon gum, was warm on his face. The cold blade of the scissors came to rest near the top of his forehead. The hair fell over his face, tickling his nose and chin. She blew it away with her cinnamon breath and stepped back.

He opened his eyes to see her admiring her work. She walked behind him, placing a hand on each shoulder. Tim finally looked at himself in the mirror. He was very aware of his ears. He looked like a kid. A kid with a red face and huge ears. He met Jodi's eyes.

She nodded her head and smiled wickedly. "Now, Tim," she said, "isn't that the cutest little haircut?"

Tim touched what was left of his hair. It felt strange and so did he. If he didn't know better, he'd have sworn he was not a virgin anymore.

BILLY

I went out into the kitchen and there he stood: a tall, awkward-looking kid with teeth that just wouldn't quit and a suit way too small for him. Tina, my oldest girl, let him in. The front door no more than closed when I heard the vehicle that brought him here drive away.

He was carrying a big, blue case with snaps all over it. I knew exactly what was in that case, too. A dang sweeper. And it would probably do everything but plant the garden, which was fine and dandy, because no matter what it did, I sure wasn't in the market for a sweeper.

The mines had laid me and a whole slew of other guys off last week. The higher-ups said it would be temporary, but that's plain bullshit. I don't know how we're going to do it, but at least we're not in debt for anything but the house, and I plan to keep it that way.

"This is a beautiful place you have here, Earl," the kid said. He had a high-pitched voice and didn't talk real plain.

Tina must have told him my name. She has a soft spot for people. She gets it from her mother. Of course, I could see why she felt bad for him. You could tell right away the kid was kind of slow. Not retarded, but not normal, either.

I didn't want to be mean to him, but I'd had a miserable day and was really looking forward to a quiet night of reading the paper. Tina inched out of the kitchen and disappeared into her bedroom while I told him we didn't want a sweeper and were in no position to buy one even if we did.

A car pulled up outside. I was hoping it was his ride, but it was my wife, Janet, who'd been at her sister's getting one of those home perm things. "That must be Mrs. Hardy," the kid said and took a card out of his pocket, looked at it, and added, "Jana."

Before I could say another word, she came in with her head looking like it had exploded into a mass of tight little springs.

"I don't want to hear a word," she glared at me, barely noticing the sweeper salesman. "My hair looks horrible and I feel bad enough about it as it is."

"It don't look horrible at all," the kid said. "I think it looks very nice."

He shook her hand and said his name was Billy. Then he turned back to me. "I understand what you're saying, Earl, but this ain't just a sweeper. It's a Satellite Deluxe 2000 All-Purpose Vacuum Cleaner and it's got a lifetime guarantee."

I was prepared to get loud with him if I had to, but like I said, Janet has a soft spot for people. She was looking at the kid all full of sympathy and the next thing I knew, he started to unsnap the case.

"Look," I said, "we don't want to see what you're selling. We're not interested. Do you hear me? We're not interested."

I must have sounded pretty serious because he stopped and just looked at me. I told him thanks, but no thanks. He stammered around for a minute and then snapped everything up again. "Well, thank you for your time, Earl," he said.

It looked like we were going to get off pretty easy. But of course, the kid didn't have a ride. He was dropped off. It was colder than Kelsey's arse outside and there were no close neighbors to push him onto so Janet told him he could stay with us until his ride came back.

The next thing I knew, they were going on about the weather and she was brewing up a pot of coffee. I didn't want any part of it, so I grabbed my paper and went back to the couch. It is a sad fact of life, but I know you can't be nice to salesmen, even if they are borderline retarded, because that's all the encouragement they need.

Then, sure enough, not even ten minutes later he had that damn thing out of the case and was scooting it around my kitchen. Janet came in the room with the kid hot on her trail, expecting me to get her out of the mess she'd gotten herself into. She should have known better and boy, did I ever give her the look.

Billy told me how much Janet liked the thing. "This sure would save Jana a lot of time," he said in that pitiful voice. "Just think Earl, if Jana had a Satellite Deluxe, she'd have more time for you."

Then he started rattling on about dust particles and things in the air that make us sick. Of course, the Satellite Deluxe would suck them right out of the air and it even came with attachments to get all those hard-to-reach places where the dangerous particles could get trapped.

I put my paper down and was just about to stop him when he turned the thing on and started sweeping the living room, hollering over the top of it about the built-in air freshener. "While it sucks the bad stuff out of the carpet," he said, proud as hell, "it blows sweet, filtered air all through the room."

The "sweet, filtered air" was mint scented, and Billy said it also came in pine and strawberry. When he was done, his forehead was dripping with sweat. He yanked out the filter and showed it to Janet. Sure enough, it was full of all kinds of crap. Janet was a little stung when he showed her how dirty the carpet was after she'd just cleaned it yesterday. It would have been enough to make me chuckle if I hadn't noticed the look on her face. It was the look she got when she was about to be convinced of something. That kid noticed it too and smiled from ear to ear.

"Now listen here, Billy," I said. "You seem like a nice kid and you've got a good product here, but there is no damn way I'm going to go in debt to buy a sweeper when I just lost my job."

"I understand what you're saying, Earl," he said, "but let me show you'ns something else, just for fun."

He ran out into the kitchen. I stood up and said, "No, I don't think you do understand what I'm saying—"

"Earl," Janet whispered. "Don't be mean to him."

"I'm not buying—"

"Of course not," she said.

"Fine. You deal with it then. I'm reading the paper."

The kid came in with some kind of chrome contraption that had big wooden balls on the bottom of it. He started hooking it up to the end of the hose. I sat back down and snapped my paper into place. If Janet wanted to be all nicey-nice, then she could deal with him.

Billy turned the machine on again.

"Hey, Earl, lookie here," he shouted. "Lookie at this. Jana's getting a massage."

I peeked over my paper and there she was, sitting Indian-style, vibrating all over with that dang perm while Billy ran the contraption over her back. She tried to smile but couldn't even fake it.

"You're next, Earl," he said.

"Like hell I am."

"He don't know what he's missing, does he Jana?" Billy rubbed the gadget over his own shoulder. His lips curled over his buck teeth into a smile, "Mmmm, this would feel great after a hard day's work."

He shut it down, took the massaging gadget off and rolled the sweeper back out to the kitchen. He whipped bottles and more attachments out of the blue case and asked Janet when was the last time she'd waxed the floor.

"Oh dear," she said and rushed out to talk to the kid, but it was too late. He was cooking now.

"Oh, I'm not talking buying, Jana," he said. "I just want to show you what a fine job it does. Come on out, Earl!"

I ignored him.

"Well, alright then, if you don't want to see."

So I read the paper, Billy waxed the kitchen, and Janet looked helpless.

After the wax job, he took off some fixtures and put on others. Then he headed for our bedroom. Janet followed him. I heard him shout about sucking up dead skin cells from our mattress. "Bet you didn't know you shed skin just like an old snake," he said, and I could tell by the sound of his voice that he was grinning like crazy.

A few minutes later, he was back in the living room, big circles of sweat under his arms, putting on another attachment.

"'Scuse me, Earl. You might be interested in this," he said and took one of the couch pillows near my feet. He slipped a plastic bag over it and shoved the sweeper hose inside. The pillow shrunk to about the size of a shoebox. "Wow! Powerful! What do you think of that, Earl?"

I didn't think much of it and neither did Janet, but the poor kid didn't seem to realize it. She might have looked remotely interested when the dirt came out of her clean carpet, but she hadn't given him a shred of encouragement since the massage and the kid seemed to have no idea. He was determined to hit all the bases and before long, he was back out in the kitchen laying a fist full of papers out on the table and spouting off about different payment plans.

I finally gave up on my newspaper and went out. He sat at the table as big as you please and told us to sit with him so we could get a better look at his forms. I threw up my hands and we both had a seat. I told him what I'd been telling him all along: I wasn't interested. He looked right at me like it was the first time he'd heard it, like he couldn't believe it after he'd shown me the whole thing. Now, I'm no pushover, but I really felt for the kid. I mean, there he was, slow-witted, homely as hell, all worked up into a lather of sweat, and there was no way I was going to buy off of him.

That's about the time I heard his ride pulling up the driveway. Billy heard it too, but he didn't move. He just sat there and looked at us like he was trying to think of something more to say. Pretty soon a big guy in a fancy suit was at the door and Janet let him in. He was all smiles and fast talk. He shook her hand and introduced himself, but I was only half listening and didn't get his name. When he figured out that I wasn't getting up, he looked in my direction and said, "A pleasure to meet you, Mr. Hardy."

I nodded.

"*Brrr!* That is a cold one out there tonight," he said to Janet and smacked his hands together. He wore a bunch of gold rings: three on one hand, four on the other. He was going on about it being one of the worst winters on record. He was just talking to talk though, because this winter wasn't any worse than the last few. "Please forgive my rudeness, Mrs. Hardy, I know I'm breaking every rule of etiquette here, but may I have a cup of that coffee over there?"

"Oh, of course," Janet said. "I should have offered."

"Not at all. It just smells too darn good to pass up."

He turned to Billy and punched him on the shoulder, "What do you say, Wild Bill? Are you taking care of these good people?"

Billy looked like he might be sick, "Ah, I don't know…"

"What the heck do you mean, you don't know?" He winked at Janet while she poured his coffee and added, "Bill here is one of our most promising salesmen. He's had some tough times in his personal life, but I think we've got this fellow on the road to success. Don't you think, Bill?"

"Yeah, I guess."

He tasted the coffee and went on like it was the best thing he'd ever tasted. He even asked what brand it was and if she used a special filter. I was sure Janet could see right though him, but she was decent to him, answered his questions, let him make small talk. That's just her way. I never said a word to him.

He sat down at the table and asked me if I was any relation to the Hardys that lived in Sligo. I shook my head no even though they were cousins of mine because I had zero interest in talking to this guy about family trees or anything else. I just wanted him out of my house.

"Really? No relation?" he said, fingering his chin. He was prouder than hell of those rings, but he was showing them off to the wrong guy. I wouldn't be caught dead wearing jewelry like that, even if I could afford it. "That's strange. I could have sworn they said they were related to you. Wonderful people. We sold them a Satellite 2000 last week. "

Janet looked at me and said, "I'm sure we're related to them distantly. That's probably what they meant."

"Yeah, they were tickled with the product. I've met a lot of good-hearted people in this town. You can be proud to be a part of it." He took the last drink of his coffee and said, "Well, Bill, are all the T's crossed and the I's dotted?"

"Ah," Billy scratched his head, "they ain't too interested in buying."

The ring man looked genuinely shocked. Then he turned to us, "Did he show you the whole demonstration?"

"Oh, yeah," Janet said. "He did a very good job."

"I'll tell you," he said, "that is a rarity." He looked at Billy. "Did you show them the massager?"

"Yep."

The ring man laughed. "I'll tell you this guy knows how to work the massager. I walked in on one of his demos a few weeks ago and he practically had everyone asleep." Then he imitated the family by slumping down in the chair with his eyes half closed. He laughed again. "I thought they were going to buy one for each member of the family!"

Janet was looking at Billy and I knew she was feeling sorry as hell for the kid. "It worked very well," she said.

"But you still don't want to buy a Satellite Deluxe off of this fellow, huh?"

"We don't want to buy a Satellite Deluxe off of anyone," I said.

"Well, we're not in the business of twisting arms. I'm sure you have your reasons."

He looked at Billy sort of sadly and let out a sigh. "You'll have to forgive us for getting hyped up over wanting to make a sale tonight. This is the last day of the month and Old Wild Bill here was just one sale away from winning a trip to Hawaii."

Billy looked at the table like he was going to bawl. The ring man looked at his watch. "It's too late for another demo. That's the life of a salesman. Well, the upshot is no one else won it either so maybe I'll run the contest again next month."

Billy started to gather the papers and the ring man stopped him. "Wait a minute. Let's just not get in a big hurry here." He rested his chin in his hand and looked at me. "Maybe if we both give a little we can help this young man out. Let's analyze the situation. I know the Satellite Deluxe is a wonderful product. I know you'd be happy with it and I also know you want to help Bill out as much as I do. So tell me something, Earl, what is stopping you from owning a Satellite Deluxe?"

I just stared at him. It's amazing how you can know some people within a few minutes of meeting them. It's even more amazing how, in those same few minutes, a truckload of hate and anger can be stirred up in the pit of a guy's gut. It pissed me off that this asshole was doing what he was doing day after day and getting away with it. I couldn't stop him, but I could make his life a little more uncomfortable for a few days by breaking his nose and blackening his eyes. I could make him think twice about ever pulling this shit in a working man's home again. He was at least fifteen years younger than me and a good bit bigger, but I could see he was soft and weak inside. Plain as day, I could see that. It wouldn't be much of a fight, but I'd enjoy it just the same.

The silence must have been too much for Janet because she answered his question by saying that I'd been laid off at the mines and we were in very tight times.

He looked real concerned and said that he'd heard about the layoff and was sorry, but told us not to worry. He knew some guys high up and they assured him, confidentially of course, that it was temporary. Then he reached into his pocket and pulled out a pad and pen.

A gold pen. I shit you not.

He looked at me, got real serious and nodded. Then he wrote on the paper. He said, "I like you, Earl. Even though we just met, I feel like I know you. I want you and Janet to have the better things in life. You deserve them." He folded the paper and slid it over to me. "I'm going to let you have the Satellite Deluxe for this."

"I told you, I'm not interested," I said.

I didn't touch the paper. Billy reached over and opened it. He got all wide-eyed and said, "Boy, Earl, he must like you a lot. We can't even buy one for this price."

I didn't say anything. I just sat there and looked at the ring man. He had this stupid smile on his face. Billy went on about the amazing deal I was just offered and Janet looked at the floor. Finally, the ring man told Billy to pack up. The kid did it, sighing and banging and taking his time, like I might change my mind any minute. When Billy went outside, the ring man said, "He's a good kid. He'll get over it."

Ten years ago I would have probably already decked him, but that's the way it is when you get older. You mellow. It's good in some ways, I guess, with all the crooked lawyers in the world nowadays. The ring man would be in good with the lawyers. They were cut from the same cloth.

He stuck out his hand and thanked me for my time. I didn't take his hand. I said, "You're a piss poor excuse for a man. Get out of my house."

"Excuse me?" he said.

"I'm not going to say it again."

He dropped the salesman bullshit just like that. "Are you threatening me, Mr. Hardy?"

"I'm giving you a guarantee," I said and was on my feet so fast it shocked me as much as it did him. Janet jumped up and grabbed my arm. My heart was pounding and I didn't know how disgusted I really was until that minute.

The ring man backed away, and when he was half out the door he said, "You've got a very bad attitude, mister." And he was gone.

Janet and I watched them go out to the van in our driveway. Billy took the passenger seat and behind him I saw at least three other guys. They'd been sitting out there waiting in the cold. Three more guys just like Billy. When the van pulled away, the kid waved at us. Janet waved back.

I went back in and sat on the couch. Janet washed the coffee cups.

Tina came out. "Is he gone?"

"The next time something like that happens, come and get me before you go letting them in."

"I know Dad, but he was so—"

"Sure he was, but that doesn't mean we could afford to buy an expensive sweeper off of him. I'm laid off for God's sake. I would have rather shut the door in his face than have him stranded here going to all that trouble for nothing."

Tina mumbled that she was sorry and headed back into her room. Now I'd hurt her feelings on top of everything else. There was still a trace of the mint stuff in the air. I stared at the carpet. I thought about Billy jerking the Satellite Deluxe around like there was no tomorrow. He really did do a good job. The floors never looked better. I wished I could have slipped him a few bucks or at least told him to get away from the bastard who was exploiting him.

But who am I? A middle-aged man who doesn't have a job at all.

THE PROBLEM WITH MEN

The penis isn't the problem, Candice thought as she pretended not to notice the boy's awkward and unsuccessful attempts to conceal his erection. In her estimation, the penis had been wrongly accused in explaining the problem with men.

There were a lot of angry women, like the ones she used to know in college, who would disagree with her. "Men think with their cocks," they would say, hitting the operative word with disgust. "Cock," Candice felt, was a pornographic and ugly word, which did nothing to capture the essence of this peculiar and sometimes beautiful male appendage. And while the penis usually pointed in the direction of a man's misdeeds, she was certain that the problem could hardly be blamed on the mere possession of it.

She didn't deny that there was plenty wrong with men. If there had been any doubt about that, her marriage to Greg had removed it. Like every man she had ever loved, he seemed to have some dark secret he couldn't share with her. With

Greg, it manifested itself in distant, self-absorbed moods, and the ability to lie as though he were telling the God's-honest truth. He was the third love of her life, and as with the other two before, the revelation shocked her and broke her heart.

It was both sad and comforting to know that she'd made up her mind to never be surprised again and had closed the door for good on the innocence or ignorance of girlhood.

She handed the boy a large picture book containing various Shakespearean productions. She was showing him the different ways *Romeo and Juliet* could be done, other than the traditional approach they saw earlier that evening at the college where her husband taught drama. She was also helping the poor boy to cover his persistent erection, which kept pressing into view despite all his shifting and leg-crossing.

Like an inquisitive little creature popping up to get a look, she thought, and resisted the impulse to smile.

The role of the penis in man's downfall was obvious, but this boy, Seth, was proof that it was not the cause. His penis had been raging toward her for most of the three years that he sat in her English classes. Yet he was not crude or half in shadow the way men generally were. He was accessible. His thoughts and feelings were unveiled. They naturally rose to the surface and could be read in his soft, green eyes. It was all there: his appreciation of their evening, his undeclared love for her, even his virginity.

It could be argued that it was the act of sex that poisoned men, but Candice didn't believe that either. She felt certain that if Seth were to lose his virginity, here, tonight, he would still possess the sensitivity and integrity that drew her so strongly toward him.

Perhaps it was age. Though she knew dozens of other seventeen-year-old boys from her English classes who had none of what this boy had.

"I'm being a terrible host," she said. "What can I get you to drink?"

"What do you have?"

"Pepsi, coffee, tea…wine, beer."

He was flattered that she offered him alcohol, but he said, "Pop sounds good."

He wondered if he'd made the wrong choice. "I'm not much of a drinker," he explained. "Of alcohol, I mean."

"Neither am I," she said. "I like wine once in a while, but I hate the taste of beer."

"Me too. I've tried different kinds, but…it sort of all tastes the same to me."

She filled two tall glasses with ice and poured the Pepsi, hissing and foaming, to the rim. "My husband is the beer drinker around here," she said, handing the boy his drink. He was sitting at the far end of her couch. She sat in the catty-cornered armchair.

He took a polite sip and smiled at her. "Have you'ns been together long?"

"Married four years," she said. It was a short time for a marriage to grow cold and routine. Absently, she wondered what her husband saw in Dora Smith, the music teacher who co-directed the play, that he no longer saw in her.

"Does he get home late on show nights?" the boy asked, his face slightly flushed.

"Yes. Extra late tonight. After the final performance, they have to tear down the set," she said, repeating Greg's half-truth as confidently as he had delivered it to her earlier that evening.

"I'll bet he'll be sad to see it end."

"Somewhat, I'm sure," she said, "but relieved too. It's been a lot of extra work."

The book still lay open in the boy's lap. He finished his drink and looked for a place to set the empty glass.

"I'll take it," she said, and when she did, her fingers brushed lightly over his.

She set the glasses side by side in the kitchen sink. When she returned, she sat next to him on the couch. "This is the one I find so interesting," she said, pointing to a picture in the book. The boy shifted. She could feel the warmth of his body without even touching him. "It was done in Canada at the Stratford Shakespearean Festival. They do wonderful things there."

"It don't—doesn't look very Shakespearean."

"No. It was done in modern dress. It adds a nice twist. Some people don't like it, but to my mind, it keeps the plays constantly alive and changing by showing how universal and timeless the themes really are." The boy shifted as though he were looking closer at the book. His leg was lightly resting against hers. "I once saw a production of *Taming of the Shrew*," she said, "where Petruchio came on stage riding a motorcycle."

"Really?" the boy whispered through a smile.

How sweet it was to give him his first play.

She took the book from his lap and placed it on the coffee table. They continued to talk about the play, and at one point, the talk turned to one of the poems he'd given her to critique.

The poem was called "Reaching," and was about a little boy who wanted to touch the stars. He crawled to the roof of his house, he climbed trees, thinking he would get closer.

"Why doesn't the boy in your poem ever reach the stars?" Candice asked him.

The boy began to laugh, thinking that she was joking. He stopped immediately when she didn't join him.

"What if," she asked, "he actually touched the stars?"

"But he couldn't," the boy said. "It's impossible."

"But what if he could? What if he does in this poem?"

"I don't know," he said. "It wouldn't be realistic."

"No," she said, "I guess it wouldn't. But who says it has to be? Why couldn't it be metaphorical?"

The boy wasn't sure what Candice meant, so she explained herself. She leaned forward on the couch and explained to the boy about exploring what lies beneath the surface of a realistic situation. The boy tried to follow her, but she could tell he was distracted. While leaning forward, her dress had slid several inches above her knee. The boy's eyes moved to her legs, then darted away, and back again. Candice continued to talk, but she too was distracted with a strange desire to reward his innocence and honesty by giving him something that would be forever special to him. And after making her final point, she surprised herself almost as much as the boy when she rested her hand on his knee.

She knew what her touch meant to him, and that his heart was throbbing uncontrollably.

What she hadn't anticipated was what the physical contact would mean to her. Her own heart was going now, and she wanted to feel his touch. With the lights on, she wanted this boy to see her and feel her the way he must have often dreamed of doing. He was a beautiful boy, lean and strong, with hope, and an almost frightful hunger that would take no part of her for granted.

But he was just a boy.

He was trembling, unable to realize how easy it could be...

She caught his confusion and drew her hand away.

There was a quiet, awkward moment.

She told the boy it was getting late. He looked at his watch and agreed. He made a weak joke about having a

Cinderella license and it was already past midnight. Then he thanked her for taking him to the play. He thanked her for inviting him in. He thanked her for the pop. He thanked her for everything. He put his hand on the doorknob and hesitated as though he had forgotten something. Then he said, "Well, thanks again. Goodnight."

She turned the living room light off and went to the window to watch him go. He walked briskly to his father's pick-up truck. Once inside, he dropped his head and banged it against the steering wheel, as though no one in the world could see him.

Her image of the boy blurred as her eyes filled with tears and her lips involuntarily smiled. "I'm sorry, honey," she said aloud. "I'm sorry."

Abruptly, the boy lifted his head, started the engine, and tore away. Candice went to the refrigerator and took out a bottle of white wine as she listened to the old truck roar away and disappear into the night.

Then she took the boy's Pepsi glass, emptied the melting ice, and refilled it with wine.

In the darkness, she sipped the wine and thought about what she was going to say when Greg walked through the door.

The problem with men, she realized, is not much different than the problem with women, and stems from a very simple truth: It is wonderful to be desired and it is horrible not to be. The problem is the *fear* of not being desired, of fading into the background, of growing old.

The ways to avoid facing that fear are endless. A music teacher and a passionate boy are only two of them.

LLOYD AND JUDY

T hey knew of each other because they both worked at the
Clarion Cozy Inn. She knew that he was a maintenance
man named Lloyd. He knew that she was a cleaning woman
named Judy. Lloyd had worked there for over seventeen years.
Judy had been there for almost ten. Certainly they must have
said hello to each other when they passed in the hallways or on
the steps, but there was nothing that either clearly remembered.

One morning Lloyd was working on the freezer in the gift
shop when Judy came in without any shoes or socks on. This
struck him.

> LLOYD: That was about the sexiest thing I'd seen in
> a long time. I know it sounds screwy, but seeing a
> woman's little, naked feet slapping around like that
> really grabbed me. It made her seem young and care-
> less and ready for something.

In real life, Judy was none of these things. At forty-four, she
was only three years younger than Lloyd. A hotel cleaning lady

worked far too hard to be carefree, and being a wife, mother, and even a grandmother, she didn't have time for anything, let alone "something."

JUDY: If you ask me, it's ridiculous to be a grand-mother at my age. Not that it's all that rare around here. Like a lot of people, me and Rick were married and had kids before either one of us knew which end was up, and then I'll be an old biddy if my kids didn't turn around and do the same damn thing! You can't tell them, just like no one could tell us.

Judy walked over to the freezer. "Hi," she said. "Could I get an ice-cream sandwich please?"

Lloyd paused for a moment, stood in front of the door, crossed his arms, and said, "Sorry ma'am. Sign says, 'No shirt, no shoes, no service.'"

LLOYD: I wanted to say something, you know, kind of flirt a little, I guess. I figured she'd get a kick out of it.

JUDY: My day started with one of the new girls spilling a whole bucket of dirty water all over my sneakers. I was in no mood for a comedian.

"I don't see any sign," she said.
Lloyd chuckled, "Well, it's common knowledge."
She looked at him, not amused.
"I'm just joking," he said, and stepped aside.
"Thank you." She opened the glass door.
"I doubt you'll find anything in there that's not melted."
"I cannot believe this day," she sighed to herself and walked away.

LLOYD: I guess she was a little snotty with me, but I couldn't help but check her out. She wasn't bad. Not bad at all. And the bare feet, man. Now don't get me wrong, I'm not one of those foot men that you read about in the skin magazines. It's not like I wanted to suck her toes or anything. It was just the plain, simple fact that she wasn't wearing any shoes in a place where everybody wears shoes.

Judy was putting the finishing touches on the last room of her shift when Lloyd tapped on the half-closed door. She opened it, and Lloyd handed her a slightly melted ice-cream sandwich.

"The freezer's only been fixed for a couple of hours," Lloyd said, "so it's still a little soupy, but I didn't want you to go home without having your ice-cream sandwich."

"Oh. Ah, thank you," Judy said. "That's very nice of you."

Lloyd stood there.

"I was in kind of a bad mood this morning," she said. "I hope I wasn't too snappy with you."

"Don't worry about it," Lloyd said. "The ice cream is melting pretty fast. You might want to get on it."

"Ah, okay."

Lloyd stood there.

Judy smiled, nodded, and opened the wrapping to take a bite. When she did, the top half broke off and fell to the floor with a splat. They both reached to pick up the mess at the same time and banged heads.

"Ow. I'm sorry," Lloyd said.

Crouched in the doorway, they looked at each other. He touched her forehead and said, "I'm really sorry."

Judy smiled at him and began to laugh. Then Lloyd laughed too.

>   LLOYD: She really looked at me. Right in the eyes. I'll tell you I felt that look go all the way to the pit of my stomach. Man! I think she was telling me something with that look, but then, just like that, it was gone.

Judy took a bite of the remaining ice cream and said, "Thank you so much."

"You're welcome so much," Lloyd said, and then, "Well, I just didn't want you to go hungry. See you around."

>   JUDY: "You're welcome so much." It's been a hundred years since a man gave me a gift and then stammered around, not knowing what to do next.

Lloyd walked away. Judy stood for a moment in the doorway. She touched her forehead in the same spot Lloyd had a few minutes before.

Over the next several weeks, Lloyd found excuses to pass by where Judy was working and say something like, "Wearing shoes? What's the occasion?" or "If you go shoeless on Mondays, what do you do on Tuesdays?"

>   LLOYD: I was getting more and more daring with my comments. Trying to see what she'd do. It was all in good fun. There was no hanky-panky between us or anything. Just kind of flirting. And she seemed to like it.

>   JUDY: I started thinking about him all the time. Having imaginary conversations with him while I worked or wondering when I'd see him next. I hadn't

really done that with a guy since high school. I mean, it was weird, but it was exciting too. I really wished there were someone I could talk to about it.

LLOYD: It was harmless. But I'll tell you, if our situations would have been different, I'd have been all over her.

JUDY: It was silly. Lloyd Reynolds, of all people. I mean, he's not bad-looking, but he sure isn't the kind of guy you'd expect someone to be dreaming about.

Lloyd and Judy kept mentioning the bare feet and the ice-cream sandwich, these tiny pieces of common ground, until they didn't need a conversation starter. It was enough to walk up and say, "How are you?"

"I'm alright," Judy said. She had just started cleaning Room 115 on the far end of the building. It was a quiet morning and they were there alone.

"Your hair looks nice like that," Lloyd said.

She was wearing it down around her shoulders instead of pinned up like she usually did at work. "Thanks," she said. "It's a nice change. I get sick of the same old thing."

"Yeah," Lloyd said. "It sure does look good."

Judy sat on the bed. Lloyd stood in the middle of the room with his hands in his pockets.

They looked at each other for the longest time. Judy said, "You could shut the door if you want."

When he did, she added, "And lock it."

The blinds were already closed.

JUDY: I swear, if I wouldn't have opened my mouth, we'd still be there staring at each other, waiting for something to happen. We both knew what we wanted. It was foolish not to admit it and go from there.

LLOYD: I remember my thumb pressing the lock on the doorknob. My heart was going like crazy. It was just like I'd gone back in time all of a sudden, and everything was brand-new again.

Their first kisses were tentative, unsure. Judy laid Lloyd's large, callused hand on her breast. They began to kiss harder, letting their bodies press together. They fell back. Together they squirmed to the center of the bed.

LLOYD: She kissed like mad. I don't think I've ever been kissed like that. She had a powerful little tongue that just moved right in. Man, I always thought of kissing like the kick-off of a good football game. It's just there to get the game started, you know, but whew, this was its own thing!

JUDY: Lord, had I missed kissing. Me and Rick lost a lot over the years. Kissing was the first thing to go.

LLOYD: Her body was different. She was small and hard. How can two women feel so different? Even before Elaine got heavy she didn't feel this tight, this strong.

JUDY: I'd only been with one guy since Rick and that was years ago. That was a mistake. This wasn't. I needed this. I didn't want to miss the chance.

LLOYD: I knew it was wrong. I knew. I told myself it was just something that every man does once or twice. And when it was over, it'd never happen again. I swore I'd make it up to Elaine. I'd be extra good to her.

JUDY: We had to be quiet. It was so sexy to have to be quiet.

LLOYD: I was like a wild man. There I was doing it to this other woman. At work! This was the kind of thing a guy dreams about.

JUDY: My body took to his as natural as could be. I opened up and just kept falling and falling. When he was all the way in, I held him there, still for a minute. I had this picture of an empty glass being filled right up to the rim. All the way up.

LLOYD: I had the pedal to the metal. I was feeling like some big stud one minute and a cheating son of a bitch the next. Then I realized the bed was making too much noise.

Lloyd and Judy were sweet with each other after it was over, even though their time was limited. She rubbed his chest. He played with her hair. She told him he was a good kisser. He told her she was beautiful.

They decided that in this day and age it was irresponsible not to use protection, even though they did not. Lloyd and Judy assured each other that they had never been with anyone else but their spouses, and Lloyd was sure he had pulled out of her in time.

"I better get out of here," he said, "or we'll both be caught with our pants down." When he peeked out the door, the halls were empty. "Bye!" he whispered to Judy and was gone.

Later that day, Judy explained to the manager that the people in 115 had left a terrible mess. "It took forever to get out of there this morning," she said.

When Lloyd and Judy passed each other in the halls, they gave the slyest of smiles. Each felt very much like they were in love. It was understood that no one must know, and this little secret was fun to keep.

JUDY: During that time, it's like I was in a daze. We both were.

LLOYD: I honestly believed it would be a one-time thing. But it sure wasn't. It was like I had two lives. At home, I was guilty and miserable. At work, I was this caution-to-the-wind renegade.

Lloyd and Judy were together several times over the next three weeks. Whenever it was possible, they used Room 115. They referred to it as "our room."

It was during this time that Lloyd whispered, "I love you," once as he climaxed.

Judy held his face between her hands and made him look at her. Then she said, "I love you, too."

JUDY: People noticed a difference in me. At the bank, the post office, the Inn, the store, everywhere, people would say, "What are you in such a good mood about?" I never knew what to say. It surprised me. It wasn't like I was going around whistling a tune or anything. But I guess people can tell if you're happy. Just like they can tell when you're not.

Rumors began to surface at the Cozy Inn, as both Judy and Lloyd knew would happen eventually. They spent their stolen moments whispering about who might have seen something and who was acting strangely, instead of making love. And then, at least for a while, they decided to stop meeting at work.

JUDY: I think a lot of people aren't happy. I'd say most. That's why they can't keep their noses out of other people's business.

LLOYD: People are going to talk. That's all there is to it. And maybe it was a warning for us to call the whole thing off.

Meeting away from work was much more difficult, though they managed a few hours here and there.

JUDY: Inside that Blazer, we had our own sweet little world for a couple of hours. We had oldies playing on the radio. It was like having another glimpse of seventeen but really appreciating it this time around.

LLOYD: Elaine was worried about me. She was afraid I was sick or something. What the hell was I doing to her? To our marriage? What the hell was my problem?

JUDY: It was always the same with Rick. We did it when he was in the mood, maybe once every other week or so, and it was wham, bam, goodnight ma'am! We usually had to use the KY Jelly, not that he cared. He loved shortcuts. Anyway, the last time we did it, I felt so sad because there we were with him inside me, and I knew that I did not love this man at all. I know I loved him at one time, but I don't even remember when it stopped. Though I know it must have been years ago. What a sad, sad thing.

LLOYD: Reverend Wells talked about adultery in his sermon the other morning and I almost broke down. What I was doing was wrong, and there was no two ways about that. His words have been following me night and day. He said, "The fires of hell never, ever stop burning. Short pleasure here on earth is a poor trade for everlasting punishment in the next life."

"We need to talk," Lloyd said to Judy when no one else was around at work one Friday. They decided to meet the following night. Judy turned off a dirt road outside of Clarion, parked her car, and got into Lloyd's Blazer. They drove to the strip cuts on the outskirts of Cherry Run.

They did not know that a bunch of teenaged boys who went to school with Lloyd Jr. were hanging out up there smoking pot. When the boys saw the Blazer drive up the abandoned road, they ducked for cover, assuming that Lloyd Jr. had borrowed his dad's four-wheeler and was taking the Porter girl to the strips for some fun.

The boys were going to have a little excitement tonight after all, they thought. With flashlights turned off, they crawled on their bellies, swallowing laughs and taking their time to surround the Blazer. They jumped to their feet and shined four flashlights inside. They released a couple of hoots and hollers before they recognized the frightened and outraged faces of Lloyd and Judy. "Holy shit!" someone shouted, and they all ran in different directions into the night.

LLOYD: There were signs all along that it should stop. But I ignored them. That very night I was going to tell her that we had to end it, but one thing led to another like it often does. And now, dear God, now I don't know what's going to happen.

JUDY: Hindsight is 20-20, of course, but we sure weren't using our heads that night. Going parking in the strip cuts like a couple of kids. I'd lived all my life in Rimersburg and Lloyd in Cherry Run. These little towns all run together. Damn near everybody works in

Clarion or Butler, so everybody knows or at least knows of everybody else.

LLOYD: Plain and simple, we were committing adultery, and sooner or later, there was going to be a price. I knew that. I knew it, and I still kept going. Foolish, foolish.

The Blazer roared out of the strip cuts and onto the main road. "Oh God," Lloyd said. "We are finished."

"They were just kids," Judy said. "Maybe they won't say anything."

"I knew this was coming. I knew it, but I just kept going."

"We have to get our stories straight."

"There is no story. We got caught. That's all there is to it."

"Lloyd, if you just relax, things will be fine. We'll get our stories straight and we'll keep our distance for a while. It will blow over."

"Nothing is going to blow over," Lloyd said, sliding to a stop where Judy's car waited. "Nothing. We are going to pay, and pay dearly."

JUDY: Then he just stops and waits for me to get out. No kiss, he didn't even take my hand, nothing. He just looks at me like, "Get out!" Like I was dirty and he wanted rid of me.

Lloyd didn't go to church the next morning. By afternoon he was denying the allegations to his wife, but did so with such little conviction that he may as well have confessed. After the confrontation, Elaine spent a solid hour in the bathroom puking, heaving, gagging, and crying into the toilet. His son left the house without a word to anyone, and his daughter slammed her bedroom door and wouldn't come out. Elaine wailed that she hated him and that he would pay for what he did. She told him that she wanted him out of her home.

At Judy's house, it was quiet. Rick was out with his buddies. He would be gone all afternoon and part of the evening. She had opened a bottle of champagne that was a twenty-fifth wedding anniversary gift from Lyndora Business Forms, where Rick worked. It had been sitting around for over a year now, and she was sick of seeing it. She drank from an oval-shaped glass that she had won at the Cherry Run Fireman's Carnival years ago, pitching dimes. The afternoon movie was on. "Elvis Week" was kicking off with a feature she'd seen several times over the years: *Spin Out.*

She was halfway through the bottle when the phone rang. Lloyd's voice was shaken and rattled. He said he was glad that she answered and that he was sorry for calling her at home. He said he was at a pay phone.

"Things are terrible. Awful," he said. "How is it going with Rick?"

"He doesn't know," she said. "At least, he doesn't seem to."

"Doesn't seem to?!" Lloyd shouted. He said he had to get away. He said he was sorry. He had decided to get away from it all. At least long enough to think. "I don't know what else to do," Lloyd said.

Judy looked at the TV where Elvis was speeding around in a little white sports car. Elvis was so beautiful back then, she thought, and said, "I want to go with you."

JUDY: I didn't give it a bit of thought. Didn't need to. I had some of my own money that Rick didn't know about. Who knows? Maybe somewhere in the back of my head I was putting it away for a day like this. And

I had credit cards. The kids were both married and out with babies of their own. And I sure as hell wouldn't miss cleaning other people's messes at the Cozy Inn. I was going to leave Rick a note, but I couldn't think of a single thing to say. So I just left.

Lloyd went back to the house and threw a few things in a suitcase while Elaine screamed, "How can you do this to me? To our kids? How? How?"

Lloyd said he was sorry. He said he was a rotten person, and the best thing he could do was to go away for a while. Just for a while, until they all figured out what to do next.

Elaine said, "Are you going with her? Are you? Are you running away with your whore?" She sat in the middle of the floor and sobbed. She grabbed his leg as he went by and said, "Please Lloyd. It's too late for me to start over. Please, please, don't make me."

Lloyd stood there for a good ten minutes while she cried a wet spot into his pants leg. When she let go, he left.

LLOYD: I didn't want to run away. I just didn't know what else to do. I couldn't stand what I'd become. And I didn't want her to come with me. That was the last thing I needed. But like an idiot, I'd already told her she could come.

Judy was waiting behind the Clarion Mall. Lloyd didn't look at her when he drove up. She locked her car and added two small suitcases to the one in the backseat of Lloyd's Blazer. Lloyd and Judy took I-80 east and were heading for God only knows where. Lloyd was silent. Judy said that things would work out for the best. She said that neither of them could go back, that they had both reached the point of no return.

For the next two hours there was just the sound of the road humming beneath them. No one said anything at all.

JUDY: I tried to take his hand, but he wouldn't let me. I tried to talk, but he was done talking. He stared straight ahead. Cold. Just cold.

LLOYD: What a mess. What a mess. What a mess.

JUDY: How is it that men can change their feelings like channels on a TV set? They can turn off certain feelings just like nothing.

LLOYD: What the hell was I trying to prove? Every man makes a mistake once in a while, but to keep making the same mistake over and over with the same woman is so unbelievably stupid! I know better.

JUDY: Rooster was the other guy's nickname. It's been almost seven years ago. New Year's Eve party. He worked with Rick at Lyndora. He was younger than me. Very nice-looking. Everyone was drunk. I was drunk. I couldn't believe he was flirting with me.

LLOYD: Damn. God, if I could figure a way out of this mess, I'd take it. I'd take it right now and never look back.

JUDY: Next thing I knew, we were in a back room and it was over before it barely got started. Then he went back out to mingle. I got nothing out of it. He never even talked to me after that. I remember I laid there for a while. I thought of his nickname: Rooster. And I laughed and laughed. Then, what I'd done hit me and I cried. That's the nice thing about being drunk. You can whiz from one emotion to the next. You can get through all of them without lingering too long on any one. Then you move on. I wish I was drunk right now.

They pulled the vehicle off before even leaving the state of Pennsylvania and sat at a rest stop, surrounded by giant mountains.

Judy stared out of the passenger window. Lloyd rested his face in his hand.

"This has to stop," he said. "It's wrong. It should have never happened."

Judy looked at him.

JUDY: What the hell was that supposed to mean? Wrong? That's the church doing all the talking. Those holier-than-thou Baptists.

"We have to go back. We've made some terrible mistakes. We've got a lot of people to make things up to."

Judy looked back at the dark wall of mountains.

"Do you agree?"

"Does it matter?"

"Of course it matters. What else are we going to do? Quit our jobs, abandon our commitments, start all over again? We're not kids."

Judy shrugged her shoulders.

"This whole thing was my fault," Lloyd said. "If I wouldn't have brought you that ice-cream sandwich, none of this would have ever happened."

JUDY: Keep going, Lloyd. Keep going. Rip apart every moment we had so it fits into your "wrong" box, since there is no way you can make it fit in your "right" box. Go ahead until there's nothing left, until all the good feelings and sweet gestures are mistakes made by a couple of middle-aged perverts who should have known better!

Lloyd said that things were going to be tough, but that they could get through it. "We both know that this isn't right. We started it, and we have to finish it. Running won't help."

"You said you loved me," Judy said, and looked into Lloyd's eyes.

He looked away.

"Do you remember saying that?"

He didn't answer.

"Did you mean it?" She grabbed his face to turn it toward her, but he knocked her hands away. "I guess that's my answer."

"I'm sorry," he said.

"Save your apologies for your wife. I don't want them and I sure as hell don't need them."

Judy opened the door.

"What are you doing?" Lloyd asked.

"I'm going to pee if you don't mind." She slammed the door and walked across the rest stop to the ladies room.

Judy had a bottle of pills in her purse. Her doctor had prescribed them when she started going through bouts of nervousness a couple of years ago. The doctor told her to take one when she was anxious, and it would relax her. "I thought I was done with these," she said aloud, and took three with a handful of water from the sink.

When she went back out, she was half surprised to find the Blazer still there, waiting to take her back to where she started from. Lloyd started the engine the moment he saw her. She barely had the door shut before they were heading back.

Lloyd drove as fast as the speed limit would allow. He sat forward in the seat, his eyes set hard on the road. Judy reclined her seat a couple of notches and stared out the window.

JUDY: Old Mister High and Mighty sitting over there. Going to do the right thing, going to be the good husband. Repent, repent, repent! If I reached over there and put my hand down his pants, I wonder if he'd start singing another tune.

"Ahh, ahh," Judy said.

"What?" Lloyd asked.

"You said you loved me once," she said. "Right after you said, 'ahh, ahh.'"

Lloyd looked at her. "Are you okay?"

"I'm fine. I'm fine. How are you?"

Lloyd returned his concentration to the road. Judy turned back to the window.

LLOYD: That meant nothing and she knows it. Love is what Elaine and I pledged before God when we got married. Love is what we built a life on. What I did with Judy was lust, pure and simple, and trying to call it anything else is just a lie to make it seem right.

JUDY: I love the way the road winds out here. It reminds me of a piece of taffy. All twisty and turny. A candy path winding through giant hills and dark trees. I wonder what it's like to be out there in the middle of those forests at night? I'll bet it would be terrifying. Or it might be really wonderful, running though the night like a coyote. These parts of Pennsylvania still have coyotes. Which is wonderful. Go coyotes, go.

LLOYD: Just get me home. Just give me a chance to make it all right again. Hang on, Elaine. I'm not throwing our life away yet. Hang on.

JUDY: I wonder if Pennsylvania really is as beautiful as I think it is. What do I have to compare it to? We took the kids to Sea World in Ohio once, which looked a lot like Pennsylvania, and up to Niagara Falls once. Except for the water and the funny-shaped money, it wasn't that much different. Maybe every place looks like Pennsylvania. If that's the case, then it's not beautiful at all. It's just normal.

They were back at the mall just before midnight. Judy was out of the Blazer as soon as Lloyd came to a stop. While she put her suitcases in the trunk of her own car, Lloyd said, "I'm sorry." His face was hard. "I really am."

Then he drove away.

Judy went home. She decided to leave the suitcases in the trunk until Rick went to work the next day. He was sitting in the La-Z-Boy drinking a beer and watching television. She told him she had spent the evening at her mother's. Time got away from them, she said. Rick never questioned any of it. He was ogling a half-naked girl as she jiggled across the screen.

JUDY: Ever since I got married, every thing I do, every place I go, ends up back here. Maybe that's why I didn't leave a note.

Judy looked at the girl on the screen. "You wouldn't know what to do with her if you had the chance," she said as she went to the bedroom. Rick pretended not to hear her.

JUDY: Part of him knows, I'm sure. There is no way in hell he could have kept from hearing the rumors. So many things would never add up if he cared to do the math. Rick doesn't want to know, because if he did, he'd have to do something about it. He'd have to go after Lloyd or kick me out. Too much trouble.

Lloyd's house was dark and empty when he arrived home. Without even going in, he drove to her parent's house. The lights were still on.

Her father answered the door. The old man's face was flushed and his hands trembled. "Haven't you caused enough trouble around here tonight?" he asked.

LLOYD: I wouldn't have been surprised if he'd socked me in the face. I almost wish he would have. He was from the old school. I hurt his daughter and he'd never forgive me for it. And he'd never let any of us forget it.

Elaine stepped up beside her father. Her eyes were red and puffy. "It's okay, Dad," she said. "I want to talk to him."

She wouldn't let him come in the house. Lloyd told her he was very sorry. He said they needed to talk. He said it wasn't too late to work things out. After all they'd been through, he said, she owed their marriage at least a second chance.

They left the children there and drove toward home. Elaine screamed, "Stop! Stop this thing now!"

"What?" Lloyd slammed on the brakes and they both jolted forward. "What's the matter?"

"She was with you tonight. She was in here!" Elaine threw open the door and started running down Route 68, crying. Lloyd pulled the Blazer into the ditch. With the lights still blazing, he ran after her.

"Elaine, please," he said. "You're just making it worse. We'll talk back at the house. I'll explain everything. I promise. No lies. I'll tell you everything, but you have to give me a chance to do it."

"How could you have been with her tonight? How?"

Lloyd caught her and held her shoulders. "Elaine, please."

"You were with her, weren't you?"

"Not really."

She pulled away and started up the road again.

"Elaine, I saw her for a minute. Just long enough to tell her that it was over."

"I could smell her perfume," Elaine cried. "I could smell it in your truck."

"Just for a minute. I told her it was over and she left. I told her I wanted you. And I do. I want us. I want our life."

Lloyd grabbed Elaine and pulled her to the side of the road as an old Plymouth whizzed past and then braked to a stop. The man rolled the window down and backed up. "Everything okay?" he asked.

"Yeah," Lloyd said. "Everything is fine. Thanks."

The man looked at Elaine crying into Lloyd's shoulder and then back at Lloyd. He nodded and drove away.

Lloyd led Elaine back to the Blazer and they drove home.

Judy finally fell asleep around 2:30 in the morning. She woke up two hours later with Rick tugging at her underwear. He was very rough with her, but neither said a word. He turned her over on her stomach. He pushed her face down in the pillow and rolled on top of her, jerking her hips up.

JUDY: He's usually quiet, but he was grunting and sort of growling. I was dry and it hurt. I don't know.

Maybe it was because I was half asleep, or maybe I was still feeling the effects of the pills, but I kept thinking, go ahead, do it, I deserve it, I deserve it. It didn't take him long, and when he was done he turned his back to me. We never mentioned it, but we both remember it and know what it was about.

At Lloyd and Elaine's house, the kitchen and living room lights burned all night. Lloyd made a pot of coffee and ended up drinking the whole thing himself.

She cried, "I can never trust you," and he yelled, "You can, if you would let yourself." She paced, and he slammed his head against the wall and it bled. She came to him, took care of him. They held each other. She forgave him.

An hour later, she pushed him away and they were back at the beginning. Lloyd cursed the God that would let this happen and Elaine prayed to Him for guidance and forgiveness. As the sun was coming up, they fell asleep on the couch together.

LLOYD: When I woke up, I felt like hell, but I knew things were going to work out. She knew it too, but we didn't talk much about it. I guess we'd talked ourselves out the night before. Besides, what more was there to say? She did ask one thing of me. She asked me to go to church more often with her and to think about living right, getting saved. I said okay.

At the Cozy Inn things were difficult. Everyone knew. People were talking and snickering. No one confronted Lloyd or Judy and people were careful not to be overheard by either of them, but they were both aware of the gossip. It was in the air.

Life with Rick was much like before. Judy and he both worked. After work, she made dinner and cleaned up. He hung out at the Ruffled Grouse with his friends or watched television.

It was different with her oldest son. He came to talk to her one day when it was just the two of them. He asked her if the rumors were true. She told him that it was none of his business. Taking that as an admission of guilt, he said that he couldn't believe that she would do this to his father. He said that he couldn't believe that his own mother was a slut.

Judy slapped her son across the face. "Don't you ever talk to me that way," she said. "I gave you your life! I nursed you, I fed you, I was there for you, always."

The boy was overcome. He tried to say something, but when he could not find the words, he smashed the vase he and his wife had given Judy and Rick for their last anniversary. She told Rick at dinner that night that she knocked it over while cleaning. Rick said she should be more careful and asked her to pass the gravy.

Lloyd and Elaine began to seek counseling through the church. He was "saved" two weeks later at a revival meeting, and cried as he offered his testimony to the congregation of nodding and sympathetic faces. "I have done terrible things," he said. "I sinned against God, my wife, and my children."

They became regulars at Wednesday night prayer meetings and Sunday morning and evening services. When Lloyd felt the desire to be with Judy, he prayed for God to take those feelings away.

Lloyd and Judy did a very good job of avoiding each other. When they did pass in the hallway, Lloyd would try to smile at her. Judy always looked away. Whenever possible, they both avoided Room 115.

JUDY: Last week I couldn't get out of cleaning "our room." I shut the door and laid on the bed. I remembered how he touched my hair on that bed and told me I was beautiful. I miss that, but when I see him, I am so mad I could just kill him. How could he just stop it like that?

Lloyd and his family were regulars at church, and everyone talked of the miraculous turnaround that he made. Still, his children never seemed convinced. They stayed distant. Lloyd talked with Reverend Wells about it.

"It takes time," he said. "Especially with children. Patience. They will come around."

Even though Lloyd was never a big drinker, being saved meant no alcohol at all, and that fact made him want it all the more. He was even craving a cigarette and he had given those up fifteen years ago. He told Reverend Wells about these things. "It should be getting easier," he said, "but it's getting harder."

"The devil's working on you," Wells said. "Be patient. Pray. That's all we can do. The next life is the one that counts."

LLOYD: How does anyone know that there is a next life? I feel terrible saying that, but how can any of us know? And what if we're wrong? What if we spend our lives going without all the things we want and there is no afterlife? All Wells can say is patience and prayer, prayer and patience. I don't know. I really don't. I wish I could talk to Judy. Of course, she won't even look at me. Maybe she's bitter. Who can blame her?

Lloyd and Elaine's life settled into a quiet routine, not unlike it was before the whole thing started. They went to church more than they did before Lloyd's indiscretion, but less than the three times a week that they did directly after it.

Lloyd and Elaine were once again like business partners, and their business was running a household and raising children.

JUDY: Lloyd is always looking at me. Good. Let him look. Let him remember. I'm not giving him any satisfaction. I'm not telling him that everything's fine because it's not. Christian Lloyd, my foot! Trying to make the world fit into right and wrong. Black or white. I may not go to church, I may be a slut in their eyes, but I'm no fool. At least I can admit feeling the way I feel.

Rick and Judy grew more distant, if that were possible. They could go days saying nothing more to each other than "Did you see the checkbook?" or "Don't forget to get a quart of milk on your way home."

They had not had sex since the night he was rough with her several months ago. They had gone for months at a time before. It was no big deal. It would come back eventually.

LLOYD: I drove past Judy's house twice today. I don't know why. I had no business in Rimersburg. I saw her husband in the yard. She told me once that if he found out about us he'd come after me, but she said he'd do it only to save face with his friends. I wish he would come after me. I'm not afraid of him one bit.

JUDY: I saw Lloyd's wife in the Riverside market today. She made a real show of not speaking to me. Like all the other women at that church, she takes pride in being a real Plain Jane. No wonder their husbands lose interest.

LLOYD: There's no reason why we shouldn't talk. It's childish, walking past each other like strangers. Maybe what we did was wrong, but it still meant something to us and I can't help but think about it sometimes. I often wonder if she ever thinks about it.

One day Lloyd tapped on the door of a room Judy was cleaning. It had been almost six months since the night they ran away, but Judy knew immediately that it was Lloyd.

JUDY: I knew he'd eventually come crawling back. I watched for it for the longest time. I imagined it while I made beds and swept floors and scrubbed commodes. I had a mouthful of things to tell him, too. Mostly mean things, about not wanting to see him and how he had no need to be coming around since the Holy Rollers saved his soul. But I wasn't mad like I thought I'd be. I was glad he came. I'd missed him.

Lloyd asked how Judy was doing. She said fine, and asked him how he was. He said fine. They sat on the bed.

"Why does everything have to be so hard?" he said.

She shook her head, because she did not have an answer.

"I feel like a fool," Lloyd said.

"You look like one," Judy said.

He looked at her and they smiled. He laid his hand on top of hers. "I've been going to church a lot. It seemed to help at first."

"My son doesn't speak to me," she said.

"You don't deserve that," he said.

He moved to hug her. She hesitated and then moved also. They stood up and pulled each other closer.

LLOYD: That felt better than anything had felt in a long, long time. And I have to say it did not feel wrong. Not one bit. I guess I don't know what's right and what's wrong anymore. Maybe I never did. Maybe no one does.

"I have a hunting cabin in Tionesta," Lloyd said. "It's not much to look at. No electricity, but it has a fireplace and oil lamps. It's less than two hours north."

"I know the area," she said. "Allegheny National Forest. We used to take the boys fishing there when they were little. It's beautiful."

"The cabin's not much, but it's something. It could be nice. Once in a while we could go there if you like. To talk. Or whatever."

"Would you like that?"

"Very much," he said.

"I thought you said it was wrong."

"Not talking to you, not ever seeing you feels wrong too."

"Damned if you do, damned if you don't," she said.

"I guess so."

They were careful that a recognizable pattern didn't develop. It was important that they weren't seen together. They could steal a few moments here and there to discuss plans, but it had to be quick.

When they went to the cabin, they always drove two cars and left at different times. The most time they could spend at the cabin was four hours, and that was rare. Once, they had less than an hour. It happened as often as once a month, and other times they would go several months without. Some people didn't know. Others figured it out, but all eventually lost interest.

JUDY: The cabin was damp and musty. I remember thinking, "God, how low can we go?" But once we got the fire going and a couple of oil lamps burning, it was like a dream. It was romantic. After a while, I realized that no one was going to look for us there. It was a safe place.

Lloyd and Elaine went on okay, though when they fought, she often reminded him of the night he "took off." His children always held him suspect, and he was certain there was nothing he could ever do to be forgiven by them. His daughter married a sailor and moved to Norfolk, Virginia, and his son became an engineer and moved to Georgia. They came back for the holidays, and things were always smooth enough.

Judy and Rick's life never changed much at all. His best hours were still spent with his buddies at the Ruffled Grouse and hers with Lloyd in Tionesta. They both quietly accepted their marriage as a mistake impossible to reverse, but she worked things out with her oldest son. They didn't make a big deal out of it. He gradually talked with her a little more each time they saw each other, and she always responded to his attempts. Eventually, things were almost like before.

LLOYD: I don't think much about it. Thinking about it, trying to do the right thing, never got me anywhere. When it happens, it happens. Of course Elaine doesn't know and never will. It would honestly kill her, and I'll be damned if I'd ever hurt her like that again. It's between me and God. It's none of nobody else's business.

One night Lloyd arrived at the cabin by 7:30 and started a fire in the fireplace. He told Elaine he was helping a buddy drop the engine out of a car and wouldn't be home till midnight. Judy was due to arrive any minute.

At 9:30, she arrived to find the fire out and Lloyd asleep next to an oil lamp. He jumped when she laid her hand on his. "I'm sorry," she said, "but there was no way to reach you after you left."

When Lloyd realized the time, he said, "Where the hell were you?"

"Don't use that tone of voice with me."

"I am just asking where you were. I mean, I have to go now."

"You said you didn't have to leave here until 10:15."

"Well, it's 9:30. I had all evening. I drove up here for nothing."

"You don't even know what happened to me."

"I just asked."

"Yeah, like an asshole, you asked."

"I don't believe this."

"Neither do I," Judy said, starting toward the door.

"I'm sorry," Lloyd said. "Look, I just woke up and...what happened to you?"

"I had a flat tire."

"That's all?"

"That's enough when you don't know how to change the damn thing."

"You don't know how to change a tire?"

Judy walked out the door and Lloyd followed her. She said she could not believe he was treating her this way. He apologized and said that he was just disappointed. He said he had been looking forward to spending the whole evening with her, and it was hard to tell when they would get another chance.

They talked until they were both calmed down. By then it was 10:25 and Lloyd was behind schedule. They had a couple of rushed kisses and went home.

JUDY: Three girls in this year's graduating class at Cherry Run High School are pregnant. Stupid, idiotic girls is what they are. All they had to do was look at their mothers to know it's a dead-end street. How could they not know they just gave themselves a life sentence? But what the hell can you do? That's the way it's always been around here, and probably the way it always will be.

Lloyd and Judy's getaways began to occur less and less often. Eventually it seemed that they might never happen again. A new Cozy Inn opened in Brookville and Judy was transferred there. It was fifteen miles and three exits up I-80.

LLOYD: They offered several of us the chance to go to Brookville. There was a pay raise involved, but who in their right mind would want to drive an extra fifteen miles to work? I couldn't believe Judy took it. I don't know, maybe she was trying to say something because she never even mentioned it to me until the day before she left.

JUDY: One of the cleaning girls who moved with me to Brookville said, "New place, same shit." That pretty much summed up the job. I don't care about that, though. I just wanted away from Lloyd. When all was said and done, he was acting like a husband, and I sure as hell didn't have any use for a second one.

With Judy working in Brookville and Lloyd in Clarion, they never saw each other. Months went by and neither made a move to contact the other. During this time, Lloyd's daughter sent word from Virginia that she was going to have a baby. The news brought Lloyd and Elaine closer. Judy heard of the pregnancy through the grapevine that still connected the two Cozy Inns. She thought of stopping by to congratulate him, but she didn't.

LLOYD: I could have zipped up to Exit 12 on my lunch hour if I really wanted to. But to be honest, the last few times we were together we weren't getting along well enough to make it worth the risk anymore. I mean, I'm not going to burn down any bridges, but I'm not making any plans, either.

JUDY: If I had it to do over again, I'd never bother with a husband at all. I'd never let a man get comfortable with me because as soon as they do, they get lazy. And I'd never let myself get comfortable either. I'd move to a place where there were so many men and so many jobs that you would never have to stick with what you got if it didn't suit you anymore.

Lloyd's daughter gave birth to twin boys. He took a week's vacation and he and Elaine spent it in Norfolk. When he came back, he had a stack of pictures that he was eager to show to his co-workers.

After work one night, he noticed a folded piece of paper tucked under the windshield wiper of his Blazer. It was Cozy Inn stationery and said, "Way to go, Grandpa!"

There was no name, of course, but he knew it was from Judy. It made him smile, and he was sorry that he had to tear it up and throw it away. He told himself that he would have to leave work a little early one day and drive up to Exit 12 to see her. He felt that the time might be right to plan another trip to the cabin.

JUDY: I figured I'd hear from him after the note, bu
I never did.

Lloyd was given a plaque for reaching twenty years
the company, and his picture appeared in the comp
monthly newsletter. He was glad to know that he would
a decent pension when he retired in ten years or so. E
looked forward to the early retirement as a time that the
of them could enjoy together.

LLOYD: My boy's doing good down in Atlanta.
guess he met a nice girl. He's after Elaine and me
move down there. I told him I'd consider it after
retire, but I'm not making any promises. I don't ca
much for cities. Besides, I've lived in weste
Pennsylvania all my life. I probably wouldn't kn
how to live anywhere else.

JUDY: I tell the girls that I work with, "Don't g
married. At least, don't get married young." The tru
is, if a woman didn't get married young, she'd probal
not get married at all because she'd realize there v
nothing in it for her.

The grapevine between the two Inns gradually fell
but once in a while Lloyd heard mention of a cleaning w
named Judy, and Judy occasionally heard mention of a
tenance man named Lloyd. Certainly, they must have re
that what they shared together had ended, but there was
good-bye that they clearly remembered.

BUCK FEVER

The Big Buck Breakfast special at Sis's Place was such a good deal that they only served it one day of the year—the first day of buck season—and even then only between the hours of 4:00 and 6:30 in the morning. It was two eggs, home fries, a stack of pancakes, two strips of bacon, a slice of ham, a sausage patty, two pieces of toast, and a bottomless cup of coffee, all for the low price of their regular breakfast. No hunter could resist it and as usual, the place was packed.

The dining room rumbled with the conversation and laughter of men enjoying a day off work and boys eager to be counted among them, ready to prove themselves with high-powered rifles. "Here comes a couple of great white hunters," someone shouted over the noise as Earl and Seth Hardy worked their way through the crowd to an empty corner table. Earl waved his fluorescent orange cap at the guy and said, "You betcha."

When they sat down, Seth continued the conversation he and Earl were having on the way to the restaurant. "One, huh?"

"One," Earl said proudly. He had been telling Seth, as he had done practically every hunting season, that his own dad only ever put one cartridge in his rifle. "Pap always said it shouldn't take more than that to do the job, and with him it never did. Open sights, too. He wouldn't use a scope." Earl smiled at the memory. "No other rifle in the woods sounded like that old eight-millimeter he used. As soon as I'd hear it, I'd start heading to whatever section he was hunting in to help him drag the deer out."

"Your Uncle Roy was a different story though," Seth said.

"Poor old Uncle Roy," Earl laughed, "he used to get buck fever so bad. Pap always razzed the heck out of him. The first time he ever had one in his sights, instead of pulling the trigger, he yelled, 'Bang!' and off ran the deer."

Seth shook his head, "That's hard to believe."

"Pap swore it was true. And you know what happened when he finally did get a buck?"

"Broke his leg in two places."

"Yep. Got so excited, he went running to dress it out and forgot he was in a tree stand."

The waitress, Nancy, finally made her way over to them. Looking exhausted and extremely pregnant, she said, "Sorry it's taking so long fellas."

"We're alright," Earl said. "Where's all your help?"

"Everyone's cooking. My man's even back there helping the girls out."

"Clayton in the kitchen?"

"Sure, he can flip eggs with the best of them."

"I'll have to pick on him about that."

"Don't you dare," she said, and patted her protruding belly. "We need every nickel we can get. Two specials, right?"

"You got it," Earl said. She filled each of their cups and was gone. An older man who used to work with Earl in the mines came over to talk to him and Seth went to the rest room.

The tiny facility was at the end of a long, narrow hallway and Seth was almost there when Claude Coarsen shoved him aside and pushed past him. "Excuse me, Jack-Off," he said, "this can't wait."

Seth grabbed Coarsen's shoulder and spun him around. Coarsen knocked Seth's hand off of him and the two stood face to face. "Keep your hands to yourself, Jack-Off."

"My name is Seth and you can wait your turn."

"Whoo, big man," Coarsen laughed, then his bloodshot eyes focused hard on Seth. "I kicked the shit out of you once, do you want it again?"

"Try it without a crowd of guys holding me down this time."

"I don't need any help kicking your candy ass."

Sis, the fifty-something owner of the restaurant, came back through with two huge bags of garbage. "Play nice boys," she said, squeezing past them. "Old Cohen is right out front. I'll have him arrest both of your rear ends if you even think of starting something in my place."

Coarsen smiled, "No problem here. Hardy's awful anxious to get into the pisser. Go ahead, Hardy, take it. I don't want you to pee your pants."

Seth stepped inside and shut the door. When he came back out, Sis was gone and Coarsen was standing up against the wall. "Feel better, Jack-Off?"

"That's not my name."

Coarsen stepped inside the rest room, "Whatever you say, Jack-Off," and slammed the door in Seth's face.

Seth's heart was pounding inside his chest and he considered bursting through the door.

"Criminy sakes," a hunter said, coming down the hallway. "A line for the can at Sis's Place? I never thought I'd see the day."

"I'm not in line," Seth said, and left.

It was still dark when Earl parked the pick-up on the north edge of the strip cut still referred to by some people as "the orchard." The gray and black spoil piles were covered by a thin layer of snow and the barren hills reached for about a mile before they gave way to the sleeping winter forest.

"Hard to believe this place used to be a cherry orchard," Seth said.

"It sure is," Earl agreed and poured them each a little hot coffee from his thermos, "but that's where the town got its name."

"I remember Gram and Gramp talking about it."

"Oh yeah. Mom especially."

Seth took a sip of the coffee and made a face. "Whew, strong batch this morning."

Earl smiled, "It'll put hair on your arse."

"Just what I always wanted."

Hunting season was the only time Seth drank coffee. He didn't really like the taste of it, especially the way his dad made it, strong and black, but it was what he always chose to have when they were hunting. He was thirteen when Earl offered him a cup for the first time and from then on, the smell and taste of it were as much a part of hunting to him as deer rifles and cold weather.

"I always thought it was weird that there were no cherries in Cherry Run."

Earl sipped his coffee. "Mom always used to say she'd rather have a basket of cherries than a bucket of coal any day.

Said she bawled her eyes out when they started strip-mining it. Course Pap always reminded her that filling those buckets with coal is what put food on the table. Old Sam Knight owned the orchard. Didn't even have to get his hands dirty, just signed a piece of paper and that family never had to worry about money again."

Another pick-up drove past them and parked a hundred or so yards up the road. An orange-suited hunter got out, slung his rifle over his shoulder and started into the woods on the opposite side of the road. "Where the hell's he think he's going? The sun's not up yet," Earl said. "That's that Coarsen kid, ain't it?"

"Yeah. Claude."

"I saw him at Sis's Place this morning. Didn't you used to work with him at Rabbleman's?"

"Yeah," Seth said, then added, "He's a prick."

"Figures. So was his old man."

"He died a long time ago, didn't he?"

"Probably ten years. Drank himself to death. I don't remember what the newspaper called it, but that's what it was. Sure weren't any tears shed about it."

The sun had barely begun to rise when they heard the crack of a rifle right where Coarsen went into the forest. "Dumb ass," Earl said, looking in the direction of the shot. "It's not light enough yet."

Another shot rang out. Seth shook his head, "That doesn't surprise me with Coar—"

"There they are!" Earl said, as a herd of deer burst out of the woods and across the road thirty yards in the distance. Earl and Seth jumped out of the truck to get a better look as the deer stampeded across the strip cut. The leader of the pack was clearly a buck, at least an eight-point, and was apparently unharmed. The last deer in the herd, however, had been hit and was struggling to keep up with the others.

"That first one had a heck of a rack on it," Earl said, his voice lifting with excitement.

"It looked like the last one was the one he shot though," Seth said. "Did you see any horns on it?"

"No."

"Me neither."

Earl shook his head. "Dumb ass shot the wrong one."

They gathered their supplies, shoved them into their deep pockets, and locked the truck as the sun came up. Seth walked over to the trail the deer had cut in the snow. The tracks were sprinkled with drops of blood. Earl came up behind him as Seth pointed to something green and slimy mixed in with the blood. "What's that?"

"Half-digested food," Earl said. "Looks like he gut-shot it."

Seth looked in the direction the deer came from. "He's not tracking it."

"Careless bastard probably figured out he shot the doe." Earl shook his head. He looked over the wooded hillside across the road. "Do you want to work the top or the bottom?"

Seth was still looking at the trail of blood. "Top, I guess. I might stop off at that tree stand we put up a few years ago."

"That's a good spot. If I put anything out, it'll probably go up over and you might get a shot."

Seth and Earl started across the road and began loading their rifles when a long cry echoed from the opposite end of the strip cut. They both stopped and looked in the direction of it.

After a moment, Earl said, "Coarsen's deer."

Seth looked at his dad in disbelief. "I never heard a deer make a sound like that."

"They will once in while if they're hurt bad enough. It's probably a young one. Dang shame," Earl said, and resumed loading his rifle.

The deer cried again. This time the moan was longer and more strained. "We should probably put it out of its misery, shouldn't we?" Seth asked.

Earl looked at him and grinned.

"What?"

"Old soft-touch Seth."

Seth couldn't help but return the smile. "Don't start that again."

"Nothing to be ashamed of. There were a lot of softies on your mom's side. That's probably where you got it."

"It doesn't have anything to do with being soft. I'm just saying, if we could do something, we should, that's all."

Earl nodded and let the smile drift from his face. "Kidding aside," he said, "there isn't much we can do. Game wardens are all over the place on the first couple of days and if they catch you shooting a doe in buck season, they're not going to care why you did it. They'll just give you one hell of a big fine and take your license."

"Coarsen got away with it."

"Coarsen's not claiming it. Besides, even if you didn't get caught, that deer wouldn't just sit there and wait for you to come and finish it off. It might take you all day to track it down. And the meat'll still go to waste because you can't legally tag it."

"Yeah, I suppose," Seth said.

"One of us will probably run into a game warden sooner or later and we can tell them about it."

"Will they hunt it down?"

"Maybe. Depends on the game warden. They're the only ones who could legally drag it out, though." Earl looked at his watch. "We better get a move on. If I don't see you before noon, start circling back and we'll meet at the truck."

Seth nodded.

"Watch yourself. It can get confusing back in there. A guy can get lost pretty dang easy."

Seth started into the woods on the opposite side of the road. He was halfway up the steep hillside when the deer began to cry again. Even though he was further away, the moan was somehow more pitiful, more awful as it echoed through the hollow. He slung his rifle across his back so he could climb faster and used small trees to pull himself up the steepening grade. His quickened pace caused a lot of noise and ruined any possibility of sneaking up on a buck, but he didn't care about that. The important thing was to get far enough away from the injured animal that he could no longer hear its cries.

Seth knew his dad was only trying to lighten things up by teasing him about the "soft-touch" stuff, but he also knew that his real problem was an imagination that wouldn't shut off. Even though he thought it was ridiculous, he couldn't help replaying what the morning must have been like for this deer.

Snow from the night before had covered everything. The doe was probably looking for food, he thought, with the rest of the herd. Even though she was young, she must have sensed that it wasn't a normal day, that more cars than ever were moving along the roads surrounding the woods. Then there would have been a sudden blast, tremendous pain, and she would have found herself running blindly through the trees, struggling to keep up with the others, falling further and further behind, until she lost them completely. The day ahead of her would be a long, torturous one and when the sun went down...

All because Coarsen was an asshole, Seth thought. The sorrow he felt for the deer burned into hatred as he pulled himself upward, breathing heavily, slipping in the snow, the trigger guard of the rifle digging into his back, knowing that Coarsen didn't give a shit about what he'd done. If he thought about it at all, it would be a big joke.

Even though Seth never knew Coarsen's old man, he was glad that he drank himself to death and he wished Coarsen would do the world a similar favor. He heard the deer bawl again as he reached the crest of the hill, but knew as he went down the other side that the sad sound would no longer reach his ears. He was thankful for that at least.

Earl hadn't planned to follow the bloody trail of Coarsen's deer, but the look on Seth's face as he walked away from him earlier didn't leave much choice. Of the two of them, Earl would stand a better chance of talking his way out of a fine. Game wardens usually acted like they had a stick up their ass and enjoyed showing off by being tough on young guys. Earl didn't have much time for them, but sure wouldn't have minded running into one at that particular moment. He would hand the job off in a heartbeat and get on with the buck hunting that he came out to do. He was missing the best hours of the entire season, but it would be worth it if he could tell old soft-touch Seth when they met for lunch that the deer was out of its misery.

Despite what he'd told the boy, Earl was pretty sure he wouldn't have to track the deer for long. Judging by the animal's cry, it was hurt badly and was probably lying down, trying to hide somewhere nearby. If that was the case, he might sneak up on it and get a quick shot before it would be gone again.

Earl wasn't on the trail too long when he noticed a place where the deer had fallen. There was a huge spot of blood, so it must have laid there for a moment before getting up. He had a feeling that the doe was close by, so he slipped his rifle from his shoulder and began moving slowly, barely breathing.

The tree stand that Seth and Earl had built was very high off the ground. Seth wanted it that way. He liked being up high and looking down. It reminded him of writing: climbing out of the world long enough to look at things and think about them. It made life readable, almost understandable, instead of being a bunch of unrelated things just banging around meaninglessly.

He relaxed into the old, weatherworn chair, while his 30-30 leaned against the tree. The day was beautiful: crisp and cold and bright, without a breath of wind.

Seth wondered how he was ever going to get out of Cherry Run. Where could he go and how would he get there?

It was easy when he was in school to dream about leaving, but graduation was six months ago and he was penniless. He had sent job applications everywhere and had applied for all kinds of college scholarships, but every time the phone rang it was for someone else and when the mail didn't bring any news, he got less and less hopeful.

He thought how ridiculous he must look sitting in the tree stand, wearing a hunting suit with a loaded rifle by his side, as if he took the whole thing seriously. Although he had enjoyed hunting when he was younger, for the past couple of years it was more about sharing a thermos of coffee with his dad and talking about things that never seemed to come up around the house than it was about hunting. Even when he was younger, he suspected that it had more to do with being considered man enough to go than anything else.

He was watching a squirrel jump from one tree to another when there was a rustling in the red brush far below him. He didn't bother to reach for his rifle, but watched the brush with idle curiosity. Then he saw a flash of fluorescent orange. It was a man making all the racket. The guy came into the small clearing for a breather and leaned against a tree. Even from such a distance, Seth recognized him: Claude Coarsen.

Nearly three miles away, Earl was closing in on the wounded doe. When it let out another long, pitiful moan, he knew it was no more than fifty yards away in a thick clump of pine trees. He had to stay still for a while, then take a soft step forward, and wait some more.

As he did this, he remembered the very first time he'd crept up on wounded game. It was a grouse. He was just a boy, maybe twelve years old. It was the first live thing he'd ever shot and he had done a poor job of it, hitting the bird in the wing, but not killing it. Even as a boy, he knew he couldn't shoot such small game a second time without ruining all the meat, so he stalked it with his knife. The bird was not easy to catch and was much stronger that he had imagined. It flopped out of his hands again and again before he finally sliced its neck. When it was over, he was crying, splattered in blood and feathers.

Earl hadn't thought of this in years. Many, many years. He'd never told another living soul about it and probably never would. He'd cleaned himself in a stream and then took the bird home. His family made a big fuss over him and his dad was proud. It was a special thing to have meat in the middle of the week, and for the first time, he got to be the big hero.

The deer cried again and Earl took another step, slowly inching his way closer to the pines. He stood very still and thought of Seth's face that morning. It was really something, Earl thought, how things that were buried deep inside of him, things that he ignored and refused to talk about, somehow showed up in his boy, stronger and more developed. Even Seth's desire to see the world he got honestly, though Earl had barely been out of Pennsylvania.

The doe suddenly burst out of the pine patch and into the open. Its eyes were wild and full of agony as it charged one way and then another, its back and stomach caked with blood. Apparently Coarsen had hit it in the hindquarter as well. Earl couldn't get a clear shot before the deer jumped into a thicket and ran back toward the strip cut. He knew it couldn't go far before having to stop again, so he quickly followed its tracks.

Coarsen's head and shoulders appeared through the scope of Seth's 30-30. He rested the cross hairs on Coarsen's wind-burned ear and watched him for a while.

Coarsen took pot from a plastic bag and easily rolled it into a cigarette paper, as though he were alone in the woods without a care in the world. He lit the crooked joint and inhaled deeply. His face twisted as he held the smoke in his lungs. The way he squinted his eyes took Seth's mind back to the initiation in the tree patch. The day Coarsen kicked him again and again. "You remember your mommy's cunt?"

Seth clicked off the safety. Just like that. The angry, red dot glared at him.

He wasn't breathing. His could hear the thumping of his heart increase. There was a pressure behind his eyes, a tightening in his throat. His face was hot. The trigger was cold against his finger.

All he had to do was move that finger one quarter of an inch, and Claude Coarsen, that good-for-nothing bastard, would cease to exist. A bloody pile of meat on the ground. It wasn't like he didn't deserve it. It wasn't like he had anything of value to offer anyone.

Hunting accidents happened every year, dozens of them across the state. The brush was thick. Even a good kid like Seth Hardy could get overexcited, thinking he saw something that wasn't there, and make a terrible mistake.

Buck fever.

There couldn't possibly be anything wrong with ridding the world of hateful trash like Claude Coarsen. He prepared himself to witness Coarsen's head exploding like a watermelon dropped off a roof.

Earl couldn't believe his eyes when he stepped out of the woods and onto the strip cut. The deer was standing broadside, right in the middle of the spoil pile. Delirious. The animal's mouth hung open. Harsh, white clouds of breath audibly gushed into the cold air. The wildness was gone from its eyes and what remained was an emptiness, a sadness.

Earl brought the rifle to his shoulder and put the cross hairs over the deer's heart. "Sorry, old girl," he whispered. "It's not supposed to be this way."

He squeezed the trigger.

Seth's aim was steady.

Earl would know it wasn't an accident. But he would never tell.

"Let the gun surprise you when it goes off," his father told him the first time he ever shot the rifle at a paper target.

The surprise, however, wasn't the report of the rifle, but the loss of the desire to do it.

The fever began to cool. The urge simply began to pass, and Seth decided to let it go. He lowered the gun, let out a long breath, and put the safety back on. He stood there for a long time and watched, until Coarsen finally wandered away through the woods.

Claude Coarsen didn't know that the only reason he continued to live was because Seth Hardy decided to allow it.

Claude Coarsen would never know.

Seth Hardy would never forget.

HERCULES

Hercules didn't have a tooth in his head, Earl noticed as the door opened.

"Come on in, Earl," Hercules said.

"Holy balls, what the hell happened to your teeth?"

"They were rotten," he said. "Hurting like a bitch, so I yanked 'em."

"It sure is a pretty sight."

Hercules burst into a lip-flapping laugh and gave Earl a light punch on the arm. "Fuck you! Get your ass in here and fix my TV."

The trailer smelled of bacon, motor oil, and sweat. Earl stepped over a transmission that was scattered across the kitchen floor. "This looks nice, Hercules."

"That damned truck," Hercules said. "I'd like to hoop it over the hill. Something breaks on it every other day. Can I get you a beer?"

"Sure."

Hercules pulled two out of the fridge and handed one to Earl. Plain white cans with big black letters: BEER. Earl wiped the top of the can with his shirt when Hercules wasn't looking, and cracked it open.

"This generic stuff is good," Hercules said, as serious as hell. "A guy wouldn't think it would be, but it is."

Earl imagined Hercules doing a commercial for generic beer and laughed. Poor Hercules, he thought, as if he wasn't ugly enough *with* teeth.

They were the same age and went to school together as long as Hercules went to school, which was up to ninth or tenth grade. Earl was the one who hung the nickname on him. He was being sarcastic, of course, because Hercules was as skinny as a rail. In gym class, the kids made fun of him because you could count all of his ribs and see the joints working in his knees and elbows. He still looked the same, except for the lines on his face and his thinning hair.

By the time he'd become the garbage man for most of Cherry Run, no one called him anything but Hercules. He'd sling the stinking bags into the truck and jump on the back like a wild man. "Let 'er rip," he'd shout into the early morning, and the truck would move on to the next house.

"People are trying to sleep, Hercules!" someone would shout out of a window.

"Sorry!" he'd shout back, and restrain himself for about ten or fifteen minutes.

The TV was an old console. Earl had given him a good deal on it five or so years ago, not long after he had taken up television repair. When the mines laid him off, it was mighty slim pickings around the area. Some guys were stupid enough to think things would pick back up. Earl knew they wouldn't.

He saw an ad for a correspondence course in the back of a magazine. He was always good with radios and stuff, so he checked into it. It seemed like a good deal. Cheaper than school. He enrolled, studied everything that came through the mail, took the tests, and got a certificate. By the time his unemployment checks and measly savings were gone, his basement was full of TV sets. A few years later, he rented a little shop in town, and he'd been there ever since.

Half of the other guys who were laid off with him ended up on welfare. Earl said the hell with that. The day he couldn't pull his own weight and take care of his family was the day he'd bite the barrel of his deer rifle and, as Hercules would say, "Let 'er rip."

"What's it doing?" Earl clicked on the TV.

"Sound, but no picture."

"Oh, no."

"What?"

"Your picture tube may be shot, but let me shut it down and take a better look."

"Is a new picture tube costly?"

"Does a bear shit in the woods?"

"Ah, fuck! Can't win for losing."

"Things been rough lately?"

"Oh, yeah. Always are. Can't win for losing," he said again. He was quiet for a minute. "Well, we'll have to figure out something. I couldn't stand to go without a TV. Neither could the old lady. You heard about her, ain't you?"

"What's that?"

"She's got the cancer."

"You're shitting me. Ruthie?"

"I wish I was. Got it bad."

"That's a shame."

"It is. Don't know what I'd do if something bad happened."

Ruthie came into the room. Earl peeked up over the TV at her. "Hey Ruthie."

"Hey Earl. I thought I heard someone out here." She was wearing a faded floral dress that was dirty and tattered on the ends. A jet-black wig sat lopsided on her head. Her eyebrows were drawn on with black eyeliner.

"Earl didn't know you had the cancer," Hercules said.

"I thought everyone knew," she said. "You like my new hairdo?" She made a laughing sound.

"Pretty snazzy."

"That chemical therapy stuff. They say it helps, but it makes me sick as a dog."

"Where is the trouble at?"

"Breasts."

Hercules reached over and lifted one of them up. "Her tits are like a bag a rocks," he said. "Hard. Ain't they, hon?"

"Yep. Don't even feel like mine no more."

Hercules let the breast drop.

Ruthie slapped her husband's hand. "Ouch, you goon!"

"Sorry," he said.

"For cripe's sake, Hercules." Earl smiled at Ruthie. "Tell him to keep his hands to himself, huh?"

"Damn right," she said as Earl sunk back behind the TV, shaking his head.

No one said anything for a while.

"It's the picture tube," Earl said.

Hercules let out a sigh and his face looked like a flat tire. "Son of a bitch."

"Gonna cost a lot?" Ruthie sounded frightened.

Hercules said, "Does a bear shit in the woods?"

"Huh?"

"Does a bear shit in the woods, I said!"

"What the hell are you talking about?"

"Nothing. Forget it."

"Is it gonna cost a lot, Earl?"

"Oh yeah."

"How much?"

"About as much as another TV, which is what I'd suggest."

"Holy shit," Hercules said. "When you said costly, I didn't know you meant that costly. How can a tube cost so much?"

Earl came around to the front of the TV. "This whole piece is the picture tube." He ran his finger across the screen, leaving a trail through the dust. "You'd be foolish to buy a new one for an old TV."

"So it's shot?"

"Yep," Earl said.

"It's not that old, is it?" Ruthie said.

Earl suddenly felt a wave of sadness when he looked at Ruthie. There she was with that ridiculous-looking wig, talking about breast cancer like the weather, but dang near in tears over the television set.

"It's old by today's standards," he said. "Nowadays, things are made to break so they can keep selling you new ones. Everything's made that way. That's big business."

"I couldn't stand to be without a TV," Ruthie said. "Especially not now. I got so much time on my hands, always having to lay around."

Hercules put his hand on his hip. "Well, we're screwed! We're just screwed, that's all!"

"Now don't go getting all worked up," Ruthie said.

"Damn hospital," Hercules said to Earl, who was putting the screws back into the TV. "You wouldn't believe what they charge for stuff."

"Bunch of swindlers, huh?"

"Shit yeah. They take everything. Every damn thing. And every day she goes back, the bill goes up."

"It ain't my fault," Ruthie shouted.

"I never said it was. I ain't mad at you," Hercules said, using his hands to make the point and spilling a little beer. "It's the damn hospital. They take everything a guy has. So he can't even fix his TV or his truck."

Ruthie threw her hands up. "Then I just won't go back."

"You have to go back."

"Why? They don't make me feel better, anyway."

"Because you have to!"

"Why?"

"Cause you'll die if you don't."

"I'm going to die anyway!"

"Don't you even—" Hercules lost his words and whaled his beer into the kitchen. It slammed into the sink and bounced out, spraying foam everywhere. "Arrrrrh!" he growled, and pulled his hair tight to his head.

"You ain't scaring nobody," she said.

"Good," he said. "I ain't trying."

Hercules didn't know what to do next. He stood there with his arms folded, looking at the floor. Ruthie socked herself down on the couch, crossing her arms and legs. "I ain't cleaning that up," she muttered.

"That's one hell of a way for a person to talk, ain't it Earl? Saying you're gonna die just because you're sick."

Earl ignored him. Hiding behind the television, he began to undo the screws he'd just tightened and then screwed them in again. Hercules went out into the kitchen, pulled off his shirt, and started cleaning the beer off of the floor with it. Earl gathered up his tools and pushed the TV back into the corner.

He took his time leaving because he felt there was something he should say, but couldn't think of what. He couldn't sell a TV to people with no money, and he sure as hell couldn't afford to give one away.

Hercules came back in, shirtless. "Sorry about all that," he said to Earl.

"It don't bother me," Earl shrugged.

"I'm screwed now." He nodded at Ruthie. "She ain't going to talk to me now for a dog's age, and I ain't even got a TV to watch."

Earl unzipped his bag of tools and zipped it up again. He could feel both of them looking at him. These people had it tough, but he was struggling too. Everyone was, except for the damn welfare bums. He did have an old black-and-white, thirteen-inch back at the shop that no one would ever buy anyway.

"What do you think?" Hercules said.

Earl sighed. "Well, I got an old one back at the shop."

"How much?"

"It's just a thirteen-inch." Earl indicated its smallness with his hands. "And it's black and white."

"Be better than nothing," Ruthie said.

Hercules shook his head slowly. "Yeah. Better than nothing. How much?"

"Damn near nothing," Earl said. "I gave a guy twenty dollars for it. You can have it for that."

"Thanks. We can do twenty dollars, can't we hon?"

"I'll bring it by on my way home tonight," Earl said.

"I won't have the twenty till next week," Hercules said. "Better hold off till then."

"Don't worry about it," Earl said. "I'll bring it by on my way home from the shop tonight."

"Thanks," Ruthie and Hercules said at the same time.

Earl drove back to the shop where he had a couple of TVs to fiddle with. The back room was wall-to-wall television sets, each with a little slip of paper taped to it, which described why it was there. The place was dead quiet, so Earl turned on the TV that the Knights had just traded in. It was a twenty-seven-inch beauty in a polished oak frame. The thing even had stereo sound. It was worth a lot of cash, but he didn't know who else in Cherry Run could afford to buy it. The Demarkos, maybe, but they did their business in Butler.

He took an Iron City from the old refrigerator that sat in the back room and snapped it open. He grabbed the remote control and flipped through the channels for a while. He couldn't seem to motivate himself to get started.

Over in the corner sat the thirteen-inch he'd just sold to Hercules and Ruthie. It was plastic, and covered with dust.

"Damn it," he said aloud. He thought of Hercules throwing his beer across the room and Ruthie talking about "chemical" therapy. "She's done," he said to himself. "Be deader than a hammer before you know it."

The front door opened. "Anyone here?"

"What do you need?" Earl said, setting his beer down.

It was the Smith boy. "Hey Earl."

"Hey Dean. Here to pick up your mom's TV?"

"Yeah." The kid usually had kinky red hair. Today it was the color of coffee with milk and it was straight. It looked like a cheap hat.

"The TV's back here. What the hell did you do to your hair?"

The kid's ears turned red. He shrugged. He didn't want to talk about it. Earl grabbed one end of the television and Dean grabbed the other. They carried it out to an old Dodge van and lifted it through the open side door. "Your mom already paid for it," Earl said. "Thanks."

"Sure," Dean said, climbing into the cab.

Earl said to himself, "Shit." Then, "Hey Dean. Would you give me a hand for a minute before you go?"

"Sure."

Earl opened the tailgate of his truck and led Dean into the back room of the shop. He shut off the big television set, unplugged it, and tossed the cord and the remote on top of it.

"Wow," Dean said. "Who bought this monster?"

"Hercules."

"The garbage man?"

They each grabbed an end and shuffled out to the truck. "Hell, yeah. Those garbage men are rolling in the money."

"I guess."

Earl thanked the kid and closed up the shop. He was done for the night. When he got to the trailer, Hercules was surprised to see him so soon.

"Look, I was thinking," Earl said, standing outside, talking through the half-open door. "That little black-and-white ain't worth a shit. I got a better one for you."

"Thanks, Earl, but I think twenty bucks is a good deal. I really can't afford much more than that."

Earl crossed his arms and said, "You willing to work?"

"Work every day."

"I mean work after work. Helping me pick up and deliver in the evenings."

Ruthie came up behind Hercules and asked, "What are you paying?"

"A television. You can help me out until it's paid off."

Hercules shrugged his bony shoulders. "Sounds alright."

"It wouldn't be every night. Couple of nights a week."

"What kind of TV?"

"A nice one. Knights just traded their old one in on a new one. It's only a couple of years old. It's big. Remote control. Damn thing even has stereo sound."

"Wow," Ruthie said.

"That'd be great, Earl."

"Yeah, well, you start slacking, the TV goes back to my shop," he said, winking at Ruthie.

"He starts slacking and I'll kick his butt," she said.

They all laughed.

"She will, too," Hercules said. "When can we get it?"

"It's in the truck."

"I'll be damned."

Ruthie held the door open while they carried it in and set it next to the other one, which they had apparently been listening to because it was playing as loud as can be, with no picture.

"Come by tomorrow evening around 5:30 and we'll get you started."

"Sure thing. What about our old one?"

"Junk. Hoop it."

"Thanks again, Earl."

"Yeah."

"I'll be there, 5:30 tomorrow."

Earl crawled into his truck and drove away. He thought about the big fancy television sitting in that old, smelly trailer. "Ah, what the hell," he said, and smiled at the image: Hercules and Ruthie, kicked back, working the remote control, stereo sound bouncing off the walls.

CONCERNING A NO-STRING FLING

Seth Hardy and Elizabeth Chase were sitting on Elizabeth's bed in their underwear, sharing a mug of hot, sweet tea when they came to the conclusion that it was fate that had brought them together.

"Destiny," Liz said. "What else would you call it?"

"Oh, I know," Seth said. "And the timing. I mean, think about it."

"Absolutely. It was this weekend or never."

"And it's just what we needed. Both of us."

"Definitely. And when it's over, it's over."

"No strings attached."

Seth's life was going nowhere in Cherry Run, and for him, the fateful rendezvous began as a fluke.

Friday Morning: Seth

I was just sitting in my car after I'd cleaned it inside and out. It was my day off and I didn't have anything else to do. The radio was playing "soft favorites of today and yesterday," so I was feeling kind of mellow and noticing how the woods around our house had changed color overnight. "October magic," Gram used to call it. The red and yellow leaves were drifting through the air and landing all over the yard.

Mom walked down to the mailbox and came back with a stack of mail. "This one's for you," she said, and handed me an advertisement from the University of Pittsburgh. It had been a year and a half since I graduated high school, and I was still getting junk from colleges, as though I could afford an education. Candice Bracknell, my high school English teacher, had me applying for scholarships during my senior year after I made the mistake of telling her I wanted to be a writer. She had me sending them out every couple of weeks and we were both pretty excited about it until I didn't win any of them.

"Your car looks really nice," Mom said.

"Thanks."

"Are you okay, honey?"

"Yeah," I said. "Just relaxing."

Then she nodded kind of sadly and went back in the house to do whatever it is moms do all day.

"Just relaxing," I repeated to amuse and torture myself. "Just taking a break from the fast-paced, rocking and rolling, crazy kind of life I lead."

I looked at the advertisement. There was a picture of the Cathedral of Learning, and another one of a fountain with some kind of Greek god spitting water. The next page showed the football team and a sexy-looking cheerleader holding a sign: "Go Panthers." The final page showed a couple of guys in Shakespearean clothes with swords. Under it was a list of "this season's exciting plays."

I read them, and it kind of pissed me off that right then, while I was wasting away in Cherry Run, guys and girls my age were taking classes and putting on plays. In fact, that very evening, according to the flyer, one would be going on in the Studio Theater. It was called *A Lie of the Mind*. Admission was twelve bucks and it started at 8:00 that evening.

I'd only ever been to one play in my life, *Romeo and Juliet*, and I liked it a lot.

Then I figured, why the hell not? Even I could come up with twelve bucks, and I sure as shit didn't have anything else to do. I sat up in the seat and snapped the radio off. I was getting excited just thinking about it. Why the hell not?

I got out of the car, walked around it with my hands on my hips and said, "Why the hell not?"

"What?" Mom shouted from the house.

"Nothing."

I'd only been to Pittsburgh twice, both times as a kid: school trips to the zoo and the museum. And it was high time I went. Why the hell not?

I went into the house, dug an old Pittsburgh map out of Dad's gun cabinet, scraped up twenty-three bucks from my bedroom, and mapped it out: Go to Rimersburg and get on Route 68 south, follow it through East Brady, and straight through Butler. Then take Route 8 south until it turns into Route 28. Take that all the way to Pittsburgh. Then it looked like the Fortieth Street Bridge, a left, a right, a left, a couple more rights and a left, and then the University of Pittsburgh.

I checked my watch. It was still early in the day. I would have plenty of time to get ready, find my way there, and figure out what was what. I jumped in the shower fast so I didn't have time to talk myself out of anything.

Mom was doing dishes. She looked worried. "You're going where?"

"To a play in Pittsburgh."

"A what?"

"A play."

"In Pittsburgh?"

"Yeah."

"How?"

"Drive."

"Oh my, you don't know how to drive in Pittsburgh."

I was buttoning up my shirt. "How tough can it be?"

"Your dad and I had to go there once, and by the time we got out of there we were fit to be tied! Everyone drives like maniacs, and it's all one-way streets. If you get going the wrong way, it's hard to tell where you'll end up."

"I'll be fine, Mom, honest."

"That place is dangerous. You watch the news. The killing and things that go on down there."

I laced up my sneakers and gave Mom a kiss on the cheek. "I'll be fine," I said, and was out the door.

Mom was hot on my trail with a dripping plate in one hand and a dish towel in the other. "At least wait until your dad gets home. Talk to him about it."

"If I have any problem, I'll turn around and come home."

"Are you going by yourself?"

"I'll be fine."

"You shouldn't go by yourself."

I started the car. "I promise, Mom. I'll be careful."

"I'll go with you, then. No one should go to a big city like that alone."

I put the Cavalier in gear and started down through the yard. "I'll call when I get there. Bye."

"Don't you think you should wait?"

"No. See you later."

She shouted, "Make sure and call!"

"I will."

As I started up the road, she cupped her hands around her mouth and hollered, "I don't think it's a good idea."

Then, just like that, I had someplace to go.

The old Cavalier was flying down Route 68, drumming like a dream, with Van Halen cranking on the radio. Just before I went down the East Brady hill and lost the signal, the announcer said, "Pittsburgh rocks!"

"Yeah!" I said, and laid on the horn.

Saturday

When Elizabeth took the last sip of tea, her right breast slipped out of her oversized tank top. Seth moved easily toward it and slipped the pink nipple gently in his mouth. She dropped the empty mug to the floor and ran both hands through his hair.

"You feel so good," she said.

"You too," he whispered. "You too."

The phone rang.

Elizabeth pulled Seth tightly to her. After the fourth ring, the answering machine in the living room clicked on. Elizabeth pulled his face toward hers and looked into his eyes. "Is this wrong?"

"No," he said.

"How do you know?"

"I know."

"How?"

"The way it feels."

Elizabeth's body hadn't responded like this to anyone ever before. According to her, this weekend was exactly what she needed.

Friday Morning: Elizabeth

I honestly don't know what the point of a midterm meeting is anyway. My advisor asks me how things are, I say fine, he looks at my schedule and my midterm grades and tries to talk me out of my double major for the tenth time. "I really think you should just choose one or the other," he says, "or major in one and minor in the other." By that time, I was already late meeting my mother for brunch, so I had to run down sixteen flights of stairs. (I'd love to know who actually has time to wait for an elevator in the Cathedral.)

The double major was my brainchild. My father had always wanted me to be the "tiger lady" of the business world, or better yet, a lawyer. (My older sister, Emily, had already failed him by dropping out of school and marrying a car salesman.) Either way, if he's paying, my undergraduate work should be in business, unless I can make a good case for another worthwhile use of his money and my future.

"Say, Dad, how about...theater?" I knew better than to even attempt that one.

My father means well. He wasn't born with money, and he's still not what I'd call rich, but he's doing well. He says it's easy for a young person to miss the boat and spend the rest of their life scraping by. (He used Emily as an example.) And, of course, he's right about theater. Our family has known several people, men and women, who took that route. A lot of them were good, too. Most of them took off to New York or Los Angeles, and a few years later they were either teaching school somewhere or changing careers altogether.

My mother was parked in a handicapped spot. "You're going to mess around and get a ticket," I told her.

"Well, what is a person to do? There's nowhere else to park. Besides, I thought you would be ready. I've been here for fifteen minutes."

I shouldn't have gotten her started.

"Are you wearing that?" she said.

"We're just going to the coffee shop. It's completely casual."

"It's not that. It's a little revealing, don't you think?"

"It's a tee shirt."

"A tight one, don't you think? The good Lord was generous when he put you together; there's no need to flaunt it."

"Fine. Take me back to the apartment and I'll change."

"Not if you don't want to."

"Mom, I want to."

"Alright." Then she looked at her watch. "I hope we have time to eat."

By the time we ate and she dropped me off at Clapp Hall, my psychology class was half over. I waited until she drove out of sight and then walked back to the apartment.

I had a 7:30 call for the play. Beth is a demanding role so I like to grab a little nap before the Friday night shows. Otherwise, I'm just too exhausted to get into it.

When I got to my apartment, I heard the television going inside. It freaked me out. When I realized it was the sports channel, I opened the door a crack and peeked in. As I had suspected, Mark was sprawled out on the couch.

"What are you doing here so early?" I said.

"What kind of greeting is that?"

Mark goes to Penn State, and usually comes around 7:00 on Friday nights and spends the weekend at my apartment. He never comes here this early.

"I cut classes today," he said. "Remember I told you about Bobby Simmons, whose brother plays for the Cincinnati Bengals?"

"Yeah."

"Well, his brother got us tickets for the Steelers-Bengals game this Sunday and he invited me to spend the whole weekend hanging out in Cincinnati with his family. His brother will be there and everything. He's picking me up here around 5:00."

"I thought you were going to my show tonight."

"This is a once-in-a-lifetime chance. I can go to the show next weekend, can't I?"

"I guess."

"Come on, I told you weeks ago he was going to see if he could get them."

"I know, but you said he couldn't."

"Well, he couldn't, but then he did at the last minute."

I guess I was being a baby, but we hadn't been getting along at all, and I thought this weekend we could try to work some things out. He said he'd cancel it if I wanted him to, but I knew I'd never hear the end of it if he did, so I actually ended up coaxing him to go.

We went into the bedroom and started fooling around a little, but like I said, we weren't getting along. When he started trying to guide my head down, I resisted, but he kept doing it. I pulled away. "No."

"Why not?"

"I'm not in the mood."

We went back to kissing, and he had the nerve to try pushing my head down again. I pulled away.

"What's the matter?" he wanted to know.

"I haven't seen you in a week!"

"So?"

"So dropping down and giving you a blowjob isn't exactly the first thing I want to do."

"Jesus, you're getting a dirty mouth."

"Excuse me. 'Performing fellatio' isn't any more appealing."

Then, of course, we fought for the next two hours.

I took the engagement ring off and threw it across the room. He punched the wall and made his knuckles bleed. We must have looked like a couple of lunatics. He leaned up against the wall with his head down, and I was crying. Then we sort of made up. I put some salve on his knuckles. We looked for my ring but couldn't find it.

"I'll find it later," I said. "It has to be here."

We only had about a half hour before his ride came. We laid down and made out a little. At that point, I didn't have any desire for anything else, so I gave him a handjob.

After he left, I tried to sleep but couldn't.

Saturday

Elizabeth Chase and Seth Hardy spent the entire day in bed. She traced a finger around Seth's chest and tapped it. "You're a bad boy. You really are."

"I thought I was sweet."

"That too. You're sweet and gentle, but bad. Very naughty. What am I doing with a bad boy?"

"Maybe you're a bad girl."

"No. I'm not. I'm definitely not. And I've got an ulcer to prove it."

"You're too young for that."

"I know." Elizabeth laid her head on Seth's chest. She said softly, "This will be the only secret I will ever keep from Mark. The only one."

Seth held her and laid light kisses on her head. "This is nice," he said. "It is destiny."

Friday Afternoon: Seth

An hour and fifty minutes after I left the house, Route 8 turned into Route 28, just like the map said it would. I was barreling down a four-lane highway with the Allegheny River on my left and the city of Pittsburgh on the horizon, looking just like it does on the nightly news.

"Alright," I said. I recognized the big, black Steel Building right away, and the mirrored one with the points.

It really struck me as odd that my family never came here. It was only two hours away! My head was whipping back and forth between the map and the road, the road and the map.

"The Fortieth Street Bridge," I said, looking to my left. And there it was. I tried to move into the turning lane but no one would let me in. "Come on!" I said. Finally, when I was just about to pass it, I cut the wheels and floored it, jerking my car into the lane. I missed getting smashed into by the skin of my teeth. The guy in the car that almost hit me laid on his horn and gave me the finger. "Up yours!" I shouted. "That's what you get for not letting me in."

I crossed the bridge with no problem and went up this potholed hill. That's when things got weird. There were no stoplights for a while, and things moved so fast that I didn't have time to figure out where I was going. Cars were on every side of me. I turned right at the place I should have turned left, and the next thing I knew, I was creeping into downtown Pittsburgh.

I have to admit I was a little shaky. People were blowing their horns right and left. At least the traffic lights started again, and every time I had to stop at one, I studied the map and tried to figure out where I was. I kept thinking of Mom saying, "If you get going the wrong way, it's hard to tell where you'll end up."

I locked the doors and rolled up the windows for some reason. I wished I would have had the time to just look at the buildings. It amazed the heck out of me how big they were. There were some places that were actually dark because the skyscrapers cast such big shadows.

And the people. They were walking around everywhere with briefcases, and most of them were dressed to the nines.

Now, growing up in Cherry Run you don't see many black people; they were everywhere down here. There was a black guy in the car next to me at the red light. When he looked over, I smiled and waved to let him know I wasn't one of those hicks with something against black people. He sort of half nodded and looked away.

I didn't know where I was going until I finally saw a sign that said, "University of Pittsburgh. Oakland. 376 East." I had a hell of a time getting on that road, but when I did, it whipped me right out of the city and smack dab in the middle of a six-lane highway with the other river to my right. The Monongahela, I think. Then I saw a sign telling me to exit for the university. I did, and ended up crawling in traffic again.

I gave up on the map. I decided to follow the signs and hope for the best.

Forbes Avenue was three crowded lanes all going the same way. I just followed it and went right past the Cathedral of Learning. It was gigantic. It looked like a big old castle and even better than it does in the pictures. "Cool," I said and started looking for a parking place.

I figured out how to circle around the Cathedral of Learning and did it again and again until I was ready to scream. There wasn't a damned parking place to be found anywhere.

Somehow or another, I got out of that circle and wound up a couple of miles from the school in a park with huge trees. Schenley Park, according to a sign. There were cars parked there, and I decided to join them.

"Well, you made it," I said, and sat there for a while, wondering how I'd done it.

I still had lots of time to walk back to the University of Pittsburgh and find out where this Studio Theater was. I could see the Cathedral in the distance, so I just walked toward it. It was cooling down outside, but it was still nice for walking. I couldn't believe I was here. I said under my breath, "Here it is: Pittsburgh."

Traffic was crazy when I got back to the school and I felt like shouting at the cars, "Forget it! There is no place to park here." There were students everywhere with backpacks hanging over their shoulders.

And pretty girls all over the place.

I waltzed into the Cathedral as big as you please and blended right in with everybody. That place was great! Massive, high ceilings with iron chandeliers. There were wooden tables where everyone was talking and doing homework. There was even a dang fireplace.

I imagined, for a minute, that I was a knight coming into the castle after a long journey. A knight who had traveled from the distant land of boredom: Cherry Run.

I would love to go to a school like this. Maybe someday. Maybe with a better job and some loans.

There was a beautiful girl leaning up against the wall near the fireplace. She looked like she was waiting for someone. I went over to her and asked if she knew where the Studio Theater was.

"It's downstairs," she said with her perfect teeth. A soft, slender finger pointed to the stairwell. "Take those all the way down. Turn left and keep going and you'll see a sign."

"Thank God for signs," I said, laughing like a damned idiot, trying too hard. "Thanks a lot," and I was clomping down the stairwell with a red face.

There were no students in the hall, but sure enough, there was a sign that said "Studio Theater." After standing around for a minute or two, I knocked on the door. Nothing. I opened it and went in. It was dark and smelled like old wood. "Hello," I said, but there was no sound. I kept walking, looking. I came to a dimly lit room with chairs all the way around. In the middle, there was a stage with two beds, an easy chair, and a couch with a deer rifle leaning up against it.

The place wasn't fancy like I thought theaters were supposed to be. It was pretty dang plain, to be honest. The seats were just regular plastic chairs and the walls were rough, unpainted wood. It was hushed, like an empty church almost. I walked up on the stage and imagined the seats all full.

It must be great to be an actor.

I sat down on the couch and knocked over the deer rifle. It made one heck of a loud noise, which echoed through the chairs. I was picking it up when one of the office doors creaked open. I jumped off the stage. A very large guy with a ponytail came towards me. He talked in kind of a girlish voice, which sounded funny coming out of such a mountain. "Hi! Can I help you with something?"

"Is this where the play is tonight?"

"Sure is. Tickets are six bucks for students, twelve for non-students, and you can get them at the door starting at 7:30. Are you coming tonight?"

"Yeah."

"Are you a student?"

"No. I'm not from around here."

"Oh yeah? Where are you from?"

"Up north. A little town called Cherry Run."

"Never heard of it."

"Not many people have."

"Do you know someone in the cast?"

"Oh, no, I just heard about the play and came down."

"How far north is Cherry Run?"

"Two hours."

"Wow. You must like Shepard."

"Huh?"

"Sam Shepard. You must like him."

"I don't think I know him."

"He's the playwright."

"Is he from around here?"

"No. California, I think."

"No. I can't say that I know him. I just like theater. You know, what I've seen, I like."

"Well that's great. So come back in a couple of hours and the tickets will be sold at the side door where you came in."

"Okay." I stuck out my hand. "My name is Seth, by the way."

"Nathan. Good to meet you."

Nathan started to walk away. When I didn't follow him he said, "Ah, no one's supposed to be in here until the show starts."

"Oh. Sure. Of course. Yeah," I said and followed him out.

"You can get a sandwich upstairs if you're hungry. If that doesn't float your boat, you'll find about anything within walking distance up Forbes or Fifth."

"Thanks."

I found a pay phone and called Mom collect. Of course, she was frantic. I told her getting here was easy as pie and everyone was nice and helpful. She wanted me to call home before I left. Her final words were, "Don't trust anyone."

Saturday

If Elizabeth wouldn't have had an evening performance, she and Seth would have stayed in bed around the clock, living on tea and toast.

"I wish I could see you on stage now that I know you," Seth said, "but I don't have another twelve bucks on me."

Elizabeth told him about a ladder backstage leading to the grid above the theater. "You could watch up there for free. Just don't let anyone see you."

As they approached the Cathedral, Elizabeth took her hand from Seth's.

"I know too many people around here," she said.

Seth put his hands in his pockets and looked away.

"It's not you," she said. "It's just—"

"I know."

"Theater people are such gossips and they've all met Mark."

"It's okay. Really. No strings attached."

She gave him directions to the backstage ladder from the opposite side of the Cathedral.

They looked at each other.

"I wish I could kiss you," she said.

"You can."

"I mean now."

"You could."

She looked around. "You think I'm a chicken."

"I think you worry too much about what other people think."

"Yeah, well, that's easy to say when you have nothing to lose."

"I'm sorry. You're right. I can wait on the kiss, I guess."

Elizabeth waited while Seth crossed the street and circled around the Cathedral. The wind was blowing his hair. The sight of him caused a tickle in her stomach.

Yesterday, before she even knew Seth, someone else accused her of worrying too much about what other people think.

Friday Afternoon: Elizabeth

After Mark left for Cincinnati, I went to the theater to run lines with Nathan. We met in the Studio Theater office a couple of hours before call time. Nathan is like a brother to me. A giant, teddy bear of a brother. He tells it like it is, and whatever we talk about doesn't go any further.

"Damn it!" I shouted. "I blank out in this part of the play every time."

"Relax," Nathan said. He walked behind me and started to massage my shoulders. "Good Lord, woman, you're a mass of knots. It's a wonder you can remember your name, let alone the script. Take a deep breath."

"Let's just run the lines."

"Breathe!"

I did. He worked my shoulders. And it did feel good.

"Now," Nathan said in a low voice, "you know the lines. You've known them for weeks. But you get yourself all wound up and you think that you're going to forget them and as a result, you do."

"So we should rehearse them."

"Zip it!" Then he went back to the quiet voice. "Now, what's bothering you? Outside the play?"

"Everything."

"Such as?"

"My advisor keeps telling me that theater and business are a bad mix for a double major. Too much of a workload."

"And?"

"And I'm afraid he's right. I'm working my ass off and my grades are still slipping. There are just not enough hours in a day."

"So, minor in theater."

"I don't want to minor in theater! I want to major in theater!"

"Relax."

"I hate the business classes. I hate them. But my father won't pay my tuition without them. Of course, he'd be thrilled if I dropped theater. And my mother was on me today about wearing a tee shirt for Christ's sake. God forbid someone should notice that I have tits."

Nathan laughed, "God forbid. Go on."

"You've heard all of this before."

"This isn't for me, it's for you. Go on."

He started kneading the muscles on each side of my spine.

"And Mark isn't coming to the show because he's going to a game in Cincinnati."

"He's such a jockstrap."

"Nathan!"

"Sorry. And?"

"That's all."

Nathan brushed his hands over my back and sat across from me. "How's that?"

"Wonderful. Thanks. I haven't even asked about you. How are things with John?"

"Same. Gay or straight, men are all the same."

And we said in unison, "Pigs!"

"Except you," I said.

"Of course. You know, it's good that Mark is gone for the weekend. Give yourself a break."

"From Mark?"

"From everyone. You're a people pleaser. That's why you're always stressed out."

A crashing sound came from the stage. Nathan opened the door and looked out. "Just a minute," he said. "Someone is wandering around in the theater."

I sat there and stared at a new poster Nathan had put up in the office. It was a grand piano floating in what looked like milk.

Nathan came back in and said it was just some guy asking about the play. "Says he drove two hours to get here."

"Wow. Does he know someone in the cast?"

"No. Says he likes theater. Of course, he didn't even know Sam Shepard. Poor thing thought Shepard lived around here."

"What are you guys doing tonight?"

"Garrett is throwing a party after the show."

"Garrett's always throwing a party."

"Yeah, well you should go to this one. You need to loosen up a little. When was the last time you had too much to drink?"

"Freshman year."

"You're past due."

"Mark doesn't like me drinking."

"Well, Mark is in Cincinnati. Besides, you can bet your bippy he'll be drinking."

"I'll think about it," I said, but I was pretty sure I'd go. I would be miserable alone at the apartment. And he was right, I did need it. I needed something.

I looked at the picture of the piano in milk again. I was starting to like it. "How do you find such great posters?"

"I look for them."

Saturday Night

Seth Hardy, looking down at the Studio Theater from the grid, and Elizabeth Chase, waiting for the lights to go down from backstage, were smiling with thoughts of each other.

Elizabeth silently dedicated the night's performance to Seth.

Seth watched the area he knew she would enter from.

Seth glanced at the audience where he had been sitting the night before. Elizabeth Chase was just a name in the program to him then. He could have missed meeting her so easily.

Friday Night: Seth

After the play, I ended up on the wrong side of the Cathedral. It was much colder then. I was trying to figure out which direction my car was in when some kid with red cheeks and purple hair said, "Hey, man, you coming to the party?"

When I realized he was talking to me, I said, "Yeah. Sure."

"Cool, we can walk together." He kind of bounced when he walked and he reminded me of some cartoon character. His purple bangs hung in his eyes. "I'm horrible with names. What is yours again?"

"Seth."

"Seth. That's right. Seth."

"I'm bad with names too," I said. He didn't take the hint, so I added, "What's yours?"

"Fang."

"Fang," I said. "Jeez, I don't know how I could have forgotten that."

"Yeah, really. How did you like the play?"

"It was great," I said, but I honestly didn't know what the point of it was. It seemed to be about a bunch of crazy people. Lots of yelling and hollering. It started out with this girl, Beth, who couldn't talk right because her boyfriend beat her up and gave her brain damage. It was sort of a twisted love story between these two and their weird families. As strange as it was, I have to say I was glued to it, even though it was almost three hours long. It made me mad in parts and had me laughing in others. And it was sad too, in an odd kind of way. I'd have to see it again to explain it any better than that, but I liked it and figured it was worth the twelve bucks.

The actress who played Beth—the program said her name was Elizabeth Chase—was beautiful. When she was on stage, I couldn't keep my eyes off her.

From what I could figure without asking too many questions, Fang and I were going to a party being thrown by one of the actors in the play whose name was Garrett. I remembered reading about him in the program too. He played Beth's father. Just ahead of us, coming down another street, was a group of people.

"Hey!" Fang waved at them. He said to me, "Let's go," and we jogged up to meet them. They never stopped walking even when we caught up with them. "You guys ready for some partying?" he said.

No one answered, but a few of the people were looking at me. Fang slapped my jacket. "You guys all know Seth, right?"

Of course they didn't. I smiled and said, "Hi."

A few of them nodded and went back to their private conversations. The party was on the second floor of an old building, in Garrett's apartment. "Come on in," some girl with enormous breasts squeezed into a tight sweater said when the door opened. "Garrett's not back from the play yet, but said to start without him."

It was wild. There were blue light bulbs in all of the lamps, so the whole room was deep blue. I didn't recognize the music that was playing. It was different. Haunting would be a word I would use to describe the sound. A slow, haunting band.

I was giddy inside. This was the best. That very morning I was sitting at home, bored to death, and now I was in Pittsburgh at a party talking to a girl with huge boobs. She asked me if I wanted a beer.

"Ah, do you have pop?"

She looked surprised. "I'll check." I followed her into a tiny kitchen and she produced a can of Diet Coke from the door of a refrigerator filled with beer. "Will this do?"

"Sure," I said. "Thanks." I didn't like diet pop much, but anything tasted better than beer.

"You're welcome...?"

"Seth."

"Seth. I'm Maddy," she said. "Who did you come with?"

"Fang."

She looked sort of disappointed, so I quickly added that I knew Nathan too. "Nathan," she said, all smiles. "He's a real sweetheart. How do you know him?"

This line of questioning was making me nervous as a cat. "I met him at the theater." She was just about to fire another question at me when I said, "I'm considering coming to school down here. So he showed me around, you know?"

There was another knock at the door and she went to answer it, saying we'd talk later.

Within an hour, the place was crammed with people. All the actors from the play were there. Even the beautiful girl, Elizabeth Chase. Everyone was talking and laughing and drinking and dancing. I moved around like I was invisible for the most part, watching and listening, but not mingling much. I didn't mind a bit, though. It was great just to be there.

I noticed a group of people going into a back room, so I followed them inside. It was a bedroom, heavy with smoke. A big circle of people were sitting on the floor passing around a pink and orange bong. There was a stool in the corner and I sat on it and watched. Nathan was in the circle and Elizabeth Chase was beside him. "Hey," he said.

"Hey," I said.

"Get down here and take a hit."

"No thanks," I said. "Not tonight."

They were all talking and laughing. Before long, some of them were lying on each other, giggling like crazy. Elizabeth Chase looked at me a lot and smiled. I always smiled back. She had a small mouth with full lips, and I imagined kissing her. I'd have bet anything she kissed great.

The door burst open and Garrett came in carrying Fang. He stepped through the circle and dumped him on the bed. "Passed out again. Who the hell invited him here?"

"No one ever invites him," Nathan said.

"Well, when he wakes up, tell him to get the hell out of here."

"Don't be so mean," a black girl who was in the play said. I think her name was Laura.

"Bullshit," Garrett said. "The last time he was here he threw up on my rug." And he went back out, closing the door.

Elizabeth Chase got up and rolled Fang onto his side.

"What are you doing?" someone said.

"Keeping him from choking if he does get sick," she said.

The way his body flopped as she turned him over made me feel a little sorry for him. Poor old Fang with the purple hair. If it weren't for him, I wouldn't even be at this party.

Saturday Night

Elizabeth Chase and Seth Hardy kissed as soon as the door to her apartment closed.

"You were so beautiful on stage," he said.

"More beautiful than last night when you didn't know me?"

The phone rang.

She looked at it. "Let's go," she said. "There's a place I want to show you."

They drove her car. It was a two-year-old Volvo. "Nice car," Seth said.

"My father's idea. It's the safest car on the road, supposedly."

"That's good."

"Not when you've lived your whole life there."

"What?"

"Safe is no good when it's all you know. When it's all anybody ever lets you know." She began to drive faster.

They jerked to a stop at a red light and Seth moved toward her. He slid his hand under her dress. She grabbed it just as he reached her underwear. Their eyes locked.

Seriously. Very seriously.

"How do you feel now?" he asked.

"I knew you were bad," she smiled. "At Garrett's, drifting around, watching everybody."

Friday Night: Elizabeth

Everyone was glad I came out, and I got a lot of compliments on my performance. It had been months since I went to one of Garrett's parties. Nothing had changed except that he was now using blue light bulbs as opposed to red. It was nice to see everyone outside of classes and rehearsals for a change.

It had been at least a year since I'd been to a party without Mark. The theater crowd was too weird for him to ever want to stay very long. So, on my own, I decided to make a late night of it. Because of the ulcer I wasn't drinking much. But I hit the bong more than a few times, even though I'm usually not much of a smoker.

There was a guy there who I'd never seen before.

Maybe it was because I was smoking, but he really fascinated me. I couldn't help noticing him. He was very attractive. He dressed like he had stepped right out of *A Lie of the Mind*, or any Sam Shepard play for that matter: flannel shirt, jeans, even cowboy boots. And he had those eyes. Intense, but sort of soft, and amazingly green. They were taking everything in.

He was different. He looked friendly, and yet he really wasn't talking to anyone. Just drifting around, watching. I kept wondering, "Who is this guy? What's he doing here? What is he thinking?" And he definitely seemed to be thinking something.

Another thing I noticed: He never drank a single beer. Didn't smoke, either.

My secret mission for the night was to figure him out. Okay, he was shy, but there was this confidence about him. And yes, he was quiet, but almost too quiet. Like he was up to something.

He must have caught me looking at him ten times. Each time, I smiled at him, and every time, he smiled back. It was kind of a flirty smile, too, but he never made a move on me. Never once even tried to talk to me.

And for some weird, weird reason, I wanted him to. If he did, I had every intention of telling him that I was already spoken for, engaged. But I just wanted there to be that attraction. That possibility.

At one point when we were passing the pipe in Garrett's bedroom, he was sitting in the corner on a stool, watching us like he'd never seen people smoke before. I mean, everyone must have thought this guy was really out to lunch. And still, still I wanted him to like me. Of course, other girls noticed him too. Maddy was keeping a close eye on him, even though she and Garrett are supposed to be together. (Garrett had come on to me earlier but knew that even if I wasn't engaged, he wouldn't have had a prayer.)

Anyway, Maddy said the guy's name was Seth and that he was a good friend of Nathan's. I knew he wasn't a good friend of Nathan's or I would have heard about him before. So I asked Nathan about him. He said, "That's the guy who was asking about the play while we were talking. Remember? The guy who thought Sam Shepard lived in town."

By that time I was feeling just a little bit too out of sync with myself, so I decided to leave the dope smokers to cackle at each other and contemplate such mysteries as why the hair on a person's head keeps growing but pubic hair stops when it reaches a certain point. I went to the front room for some air.

Seth was using Garrett's phone when I went in. Except for the smokers in the bedroom, and Maddy and Garrett arguing in a far corner, the place had nearly emptied out.

Seth hung up the phone and went over to the window.

I decided it would be nice to at least say hello to the mystery man who I'd spent the evening exchanging smiles with. "See anything interesting out there?"

He looked at me, kind of surprised. Those eyes. God, they don't make eyes more beautiful than that. "Well, I ah… I was just wondering how far Schenley Park is from here."

"A mile or two."

He nodded and said, "You were really great in the play tonight."

"Thank you."

"I really mean that. You were excellent."

"Thank you very much." Standing beside him, I felt nervous. A fun kind of nervous that I hadn't felt in years. "So what's in Schenley Park?"

"My car. I parked up there before the play. My name is Seth."

"I know."

"You know?"

"Maddy told me. She says you're a good friend of Nathan's."

He smiled and blushed a little bit. "Yeah, I've known old Nathan since…this afternoon."

"So why does a guy who doesn't drink beer or smoke pot crash a party where nothing else is being served?"

"Actually, Fang invited me."

We both laughed.

"And how far back do you and Fang go?"

"Not quite as far as Nathan and I."

He was so easy to talk to. Once we got started, it was difficult to stop. We discussed the play, and he had a lot of questions about Pitt. He lives in this little town called Cherry Run and said it's driving him crazy. I wished that it hadn't been so late when we started talking because there was so much to say. At about 3:30, I knew I had to get going.

We had such a great talk that when I went to leave, I hugged him. It was a good hug.

He said he might come to see the play again next week. Maybe we could talk more then.

I was halfway to the elevator when I decided that I should have him walk me to my building since it was so late. Then I thought it would be nice to drive him to his car. Schenley Park could be dangerous at that time of night.

I had no more than turned around in the hallway when he came out. His whole face lit up when he saw me. He loved the idea of a ride to his car. My car keys were in my apartment, so we stopped off for them. He stepped inside while I got them. When we were about to walk out the door, there was a moment when we stopped talking and just stood there, looking at each other.

I was in a swirl of feelings. I was engaged. And I didn't even know this guy. What the hell was I doing escorting him into my apartment? And as the coup de grace, I wanted to kiss him.

He brushed the hair out of my face and moved to kiss me.

"No." I leaned away. "I can't." I had mentioned Mark before, but left out the engaged part. I told him now. (Nevermind that I wasn't wearing a ring because I had thrown it across the apartment earlier and still couldn't find it.)

Seth said that it was okay, but I could tell he was embarrassed. I told him that Mark and I were having trouble, but we were working it out. He said that he understood and would still like to be my friend.

I said, "That would be nice."

And kissed him like I've never kissed anyone before.

Saturday Night

Elizabeth Chase ignored the speed limit as she drove out of Oakland. She raced across the Liberty Bridge and roared up, way up McArdle Roadway.

"Where are we going?"

"A surprise."

They finally reached the top of the hill, and Elizabeth parked the car. "Welcome to Mount Washington."

"Wow," Seth said as they got out. He could see the whole city below. He saw the famous three rivers, the stadium where the Steelers and Pirates played, the lighted buildings in every direction, and the countless roads twisting every which way. "Wow," he said again. "I never knew a city could be beautiful, but it is."

Elizabeth walked to the railing of the overlook and Seth came up behind her. "Over there," she pointed, "is where we just came from. The building with the red light on top is the Cathedral."

The cold, autumn wind blew through their hair, and Seth wrapped his arms tightly around her. They savored the warmth of each other's skin. Elizabeth leaned into him. Without turning around, she said, "I'm going to miss this. I'm going to miss you."

"Maybe it doesn't have to end."

"I'm engaged to another man."

"You don't have to be."

"I want to be."

"You could have fooled me."

Elizabeth pulled away from him. "Please, Seth. We've discussed this. I want this weekend with you, but I don't want to wreck my whole life over it. We agreed—"

"I know. No strings."

"Please don't look at me like that."

"I'm sorry."

They stared silently across the city for what seemed like a long time. Then Elizabeth took Seth's hand. "We still have the whole night. We could go back to my apartment."

He touched her cheek and tried to smile. "That would be nice. I could really go for…another cup of tea."

She squeezed his hand. "At least one more."

The windows of Elizabeth's living room were dripping with condensation and the air was heavy with the smell of sex. She collapsed on the couch and pulled a damp sheet over her nakedness.

Seth was lying on the carpet with his hands behind his head, wearing, as they say, nothing but a smile.

Elizabeth shoved him gently with a bare foot. "Look at you!"

"What?"

"You have got the most self-satisfied, stud-man look on your face that I have ever seen."

"Well, the last twenty-four hours have given me a lot to feel good about."

"I'll agree with that."

"And you did say, just a little while ago, that you have never felt like this with anyone else."

Elizabeth pulled the sheet over her face.

Seth continued, "In fact, your exact words were—"

"Stop it!"

"Okay. Is it true, though, that it's the best you've ever had?"

Elizabeth peeked over the sheet. "Definitely."

"Wow. Me too." They looked at each other. "Why would you marry a guy that can't make you feel like that?"

"It's about more than just sex."

"Was this 'just sex?'"

"Mark and I have been together for over three years. We want the same things out of life."

"Are you going to tell him about this weekend?"

"Of course not!"

"So before you're even married, you want lies and cheating between you?"

"I really don't want to talk about this with you."

"Do you think Mark has done something like this?"

"No."

"How do you know?"

"I know!"

"But if *you*—"

"Look, you don't know me that well. You really don't. And you don't know Mark at all, so just give it a rest!"

"You're right," Seth sighed. "It's none of my business." He took a quarter from a handful of pocket change on the end table. "I'll flip you for who makes the tea."

Elizabeth didn't say anything.

"Do you want tea?"

"Heads," she said.

Seth tossed the coin in the air and it bounced on the carpet. "Tails. I lose." He put on his underwear and walked into the kitchen. He rinsed the big mug out and plopped two bags in it while the water boiled.

When the tea was strong and sweet enough, Seth joined her on the couch. They wrapped the sheet around them. "So, stud, have you been with a lot of girls?"

"I wouldn't say a lot, exactly."

"Oh. Well, how many would you say? Exactly?"

"Counting you?"

She nudged him with her foot again. "Yes, counting me."

Seth closed his eyes, moved his lips, and nodded several times. "Counting you?"

"Seth!"

"Okay, okay." He went back to counting. Then he opened his eyes and said, "Counting you: three."

She smiled at this.

"Surprised?" he asked.

"Yes and no."

"What about you?"

"I've been with Mark for over three years. Before that, my two boyfriends in high school." She rolled her eyes. "One of those I probably shouldn't even count. But anyway: four. Surprised?"

"Sort of."

"Thanks a lot!"

"Well, you're so pretty and you live in a big city and—"

She laughed.

"What?"

"I love the way you describe Pittsburgh as a 'big city.'" She kissed his forehead. "I'm sorry. Go on."

"That's all."

"So if you've only been with two girls before me…?"

"How did I get so good?"

"And modest. Don't forget modest."

At 5:35 a.m. Sunday, in an Eat and Park, over french fries with gravy and a Caesar salad, Seth Hardy and Elizabeth Chase resolved that if a guy and girl wanted to have a wild sexual weekend with no strings attached, they shouldn't talk so much.

"If someone told me this would happen two days ago, I would have never believed it," Elizabeth said, crunching a crouton. "I sure didn't plan it."

"Me neither," Seth said. Then added, "I mean, I would have planned it if I thought it were possible."

She threw a piece of lettuce at him. "So will you plan it now that you know it's possible?"

"Do you mean with you, or with someone else?"

"It would have to be with someone else, because I'm not doing this anymore. If I did, it would be with you. But I'm not."

"Yeah. I'd plan a few more of these in my future if I could. Beautiful woman, incredible sex, no strings attached."

A light wave of sadness drifted across Elizabeth's face. She broke it with a smile.

"Well," she said, taking a pen from her purse and a napkin from the table, "we'll make a list of do's and don'ts for your future endeavors." Across the top of it she wrote, "Concerning a no-string fling."

"We've already got number one," Seth said. He wiped some gravy from his mouth. "Don't talk so much. It makes it hard to leave."

"Which brings up number two. After a night of passion with a stranger…" she said, then wrote, "Do go home."

"Yeah. I definitely need to work on that one."

Elizabeth wrote number three without conferring with Seth and covered the napkin with her hand so he couldn't see it. Then she folded the napkin and placed it in his shirt pocket.

He went to read it and she said, "No. Later."

It was past noon when Seth woke up alone in Elizabeth's bedroom. He laid there for a moment and savored the feeling of being naked in a pretty girl's bed. Across the room on the desk he saw a jar of pens and a tablet. On a clean sheet of paper, he wrote his address and phone number. He laid it on her pillow and wrapped himself in the blanket. Just as he opened the bedroom door, he heard her voice from the living room.

Elizabeth was talking on the phone. "I just got the messages," she said. "Yeah, Emily surprised me yesterday morning. It was so nice to see her. We went shopping at Ross Park Mall all day. Then she came to the show and dragged me out for drinks afterward. We spent the night and next day at her place. Yeah, it was nice to see her. How's things there? Really? That's great." It was quiet for a while. Then she continued, "It went okay. I missed you, though. Okay. Have a good time. When will I see you? Great. Okay. Love you. Bye."

Seth walked into the room wrapped in the blanket. "Morning," he said.

"Afternoon," Elizabeth said. She was dressed in a beige skirt and navy blue vest. Her hair and make-up were done.

"Are you going somewhere?"

"I've got a lot of errands to run. Not to mention that I never opened a book all weekend."

"Is everything okay?"

"Fine."

It was quiet for a moment.

Seth said, "I guess I should get going."

"I guess so."

Seth noticed that Elizabeth was wearing her engagement ring. He nodded toward her hand. "I see you found it."

"Yeah. This morning."

"Big stone."

She looked at the ring and moved it back and forth with the thumb of the same hand. "Yes. It is."

They looked at each other.

"Would you like some tea before you go?"

"That would be nice."

Elizabeth went to the kitchen. Seth went to the bedroom. He laid the blanket on the bed and dressed. In the bathroom he washed his face and brushed his teeth. When he was finished, Elizabeth served him a small cup of tea.

"You're not having any?" he asked.

"I had some earlier."

Seth stood in the center of the room and finished his tea. "That was good. Thank you."

"You're welcome. I can drive you to your car if you'd like."

"No. It's a nice day to walk. Schenley Park isn't hard to find from here, right?"

"Walk past the Cathedral, left at the library, cross the two bridges, and you're there. But I don't mind driving you."

"No. I'll walk."

They gave each other an awkward hug.

"I don't have your number," Seth said.

"I don't think it's a good idea."

"Okay," he said, and went out the door. In the hallway, he stopped. "Bullshit," he whispered, and knocked on the door. There was no answer. He knocked a second and then a third time.

Elizabeth opened the door. Tears streaked each side of her face. She sighed, "You're not supposed to come back, Seth."

They hugged. A deep hug this time, as though they were alternately holding onto and letting go of something very special.

"Don't hate me," she said. "Don't think bad things of me."

"I won't."

She looked into his eyes. "Why are you so nice?"

"My mom's nice."

Elizabeth laughed through her tears. "I see. Genetics."

Elizabeth Chase was making her bed when she found Seth Hardy's address and phone number. He signed it, "Your Bad Boy," and left the post script, "Ulcer or not, you can be a VERY BAD GIRL!"

At about the same time, on Route 8 at a stoplight just outside of Butler, Seth pulled the folded napkin from his shirt pocket. In Elizabeth's precise handwriting, it read:

Concerning a no-string fling:
1. Don't talk so much
2. Do go home
3. Don't fall in love.

WILD HAIRS

Mike's mind was made up: He was shaving his back.
"Don't be ridiculous," his wife Heidi said. "Do you want to be covered in stubble?"

Mike had threatened to do this since he was in high school. And now, today, he was finally taking action. No more smart-assed, adolescent "yucks" or "ooos" when he walked by without his shirt. No more Hair Ball, Caveman, Werewolf. No more!

Heidi followed him up the stairs and down the hall. "I cannot believe that you would let a couple of teenage girls get you so upset."

"It has nothing to do with those brats at the mall," he said, yanking off his tank top. "I've always hated having a hairy back, and I'm not going to put up with it anymore."

Heidi didn't know what to do. She stopped just outside the open bathroom door and placed her hands firmly on her hips. Thank goodness the kids were visiting her parents across town. Her father had a word for Mike: rambunctious.

"That guy gets a wild hair up his ass," he would say, shaking his head in a tsk, tsk, tsk manner, "and thinks he's going to change the world. Well, he ain't. Things are the way they are and that's that."

But Mike had a whole back full of wild hairs, and that particular piece of the world was just about to change. He kicked his sandals off, jerked his pants and underwear down, and ripped open a bag of disposable razors. Heidi dropped her hands at her sides. "For goodness' sake, Mike," she said, as he marched toward the shower with three plastic razors clutched in a determined fist. "If it's so important to you, then we'll look into having it done. Maybe you can get waxed or something, but shaving...good grief."

Mike wasn't waiting. He cranked on the shower, stepped inside, closed the curtain and let the hiss of the spray drown out all distraction. He closed his eyes. The water was very warm and a cool summer breeze slipped through the shower curtain from the open window. It was a good feeling. He took a deep breath. He relaxed a little. His mad determination loosened and he considered what he was about to do. Heidi was right. It was ridiculous. It was nuts.

But he smiled at himself because he was going to do it anyway and he was going to have fun with it. "Do we have anything to drink in the house?" he asked Heidi.

"I think we have some beer. Why?"

"Let's crack open a few and have a shaving party."

"Mike, this is asinine."

"I'm not turning back, Heidi. I'm doing it."

Heidi, not knowing what else to do, went for the beer.

The can of shaving cream advertised "supreme closeness for supreme comfort," and the contents spread evenly across his left shoulder, filling the air with a manly cologne. He picked up a new razor and with one easy stroke outward from his neck there appeared a smooth, clean, dry path. Just like that.

Heidi returned with a six-pack. "Are you doing it?"

"Sure am."

"Good grief, Mike," she said and opened two beers.

Mike tapped the razor against the tile.

"You're not letting that hair go down the drain, are you?" Heidi wanted to know.

"Nope." He was trapping the fallen hair with his foot and scooting it into a little black pile at the upper corner of the tub. "How about that drink?" he said and reached a wet hand through the curtain.

Heidi handed him a sweating bottle and quietly assumed the position of "The Thinker" on the edge of the commode. By the time his shoulders were clean, she was musing absently, "What are people going to say? What will we tell our friends? My parents? 'Yeah, Mike shaved his back the other day.' I mean normal people just don't do that."

After reaching as far down his back as he could, Mike went for a fresh razor. Taking action felt good. He knew it would, but didn't expect the other sensation. It was the weirdest damn thing, but the feel of the bare skin and the look of it was kind of...well...arousing. "Heidi? Why don't you come in?"

Heidi was still muttering, "'...so he just shaved 'er off.'"

"Honey, take your clothes off and come on in," Mike said. "I need your help reaching the rest."

Heidi stood up and walked closer. She took another swig from the bottle. "I'm afraid to look."

"It looks great," he said. "I knew it would."

"I can't look."

"I should have done this years ago."

Mike's large, hairy arm reached out to pull her closer. She stepped away. "No. I don't want to see it."

Mike peeked out. Heidi was still dressed and her eyes were squeezed shut. In his present state, he found it adorable. He took her arm and lightly guided her closer. "You'll love it," he said, and placed her hand on his smooth, wet shoulder.

She gasped, but kept her eyes closed.

"Nice, huh?"

Then he moved her hand downward. "Honey!" she whispered.

"What? It's just us. We don't have to get the kids for hours yet." Then he stepped back into the spray of the shower and closed the curtain. "So get those clothes off and get in here."

Heidi opened her eyes. She was still a little apprehensive about seeing her hairy husband without hair, but it was nice to have the house to themselves, so she began undoing the button of her jeans.

Then, with the confidence of a god, Mike suddenly yanked the curtain wide open, exhibiting two freshly shaved shoulders and one furious erection.

Heidi screamed, scaring both of them.

"What the hell?" Mike said.

Heidi put a hand over her mouth. She gaped at her husband and nodded aimlessly, "Oh, Mike."

"What?"

"Oh, honey."

"What?"

Then she broke into a nervous, high-pitched laugh that drained what was left of Mike's bravado.

"What the hell are you laughing at?"

"I'm sorry." She tried to swallow the laughter, but it came back up in high-pitched little peals.

"Damn it, Heidi!"

"I'm sorry," she said again.

"What do you expect?" he growled. "It's only half done."

"I just wasn't expecting…I don't know what I was expecting."

He turned to shut off the shower, giving her a full view of his barbering endeavor. This sent her into another series of spontaneous chuckles.

Mike gave her the eye, and she tried to explain, "I'm not laughing *at* you. It's just…"

"Are you going to help me or not?" His brain was now completely out of his penis and back in his head. He thrust the shaving cream and a fresh razor at his wife and turned his back to her. "Let's go."

"Shouldn't we use scissors first?" she asked.

"No."

"But the razor will get all clogged up."

"Just keep knocking the hair out of it."

She lathered up his back. "How far do I go?"

"The whole way to the bottom."

She burst.

"Damn it, Heidi! Come on now. I mean it!"

"But you're going to have a bald back and this big old hairy butt."

"Well nobody is going to see that besides you and me, and we're used to it."

"But—"

"But nothing. Are you going to do it or do I have to figure out a way to do it myself?"

"It isn't going to go with the rest of your body."

"Well, it's too damn late to turn back now," he shouted.

"Okay, okay. Take it easy. I'm just trying to help."

Heidi took a deep breath and went to work.

The next morning, Mike felt great. Better than he had in years. He noticed the sun shining, the birds singing. He was halfway through brushing his teeth when he thought about the sparkling blue water of the Cherry Run Municipal Pool. It was brand new this year. He drove past it every day on his way to work.

He imagined how good it would feel to spend the whole day swimming and lying in the sun instead of being cooped up in the gray world of Lyndora Business Forms. By the time he'd finished brushing his teeth, he'd concluded that there wasn't a single reason why he couldn't spend the day doing whatever he wanted. Heidi was already off to work and the kids had just boarded the bus for school. He had a pile of sick days coming from the factory and all he had to do to claim one was make a simple phone call. He even had season passes to the new pool hidden in his underwear drawer: a surprise for Heidi and the kids.

Mike called the secretary at Lyndora and told her he wouldn't be in because he had the flu. She never asked a single question, just said okay and good-bye. He decided to make the whole day a celebration and kicked it off with a nice leisurely breakfast, something he never took the time for on working days: eggs, toast, and coffee. The pool opened at 10:00 and he was the first patron in the parking lot at 10:02.

The Cherry Run Municipal Pool was an incredible splurge for the town and Mike couldn't believe they'd actually done it. Everything looked and smelled new. The men's bathhouse was spacious, with shiny lockers, wooden benches, group and individual showers, the whole works.

Since school hadn't let out yet, Mike practically had the place to himself. He was alone in the bathhouse and took advantage of the full-length mirror. It was nice to see hairless shoulders and a broad, bald back. Heidi had suggested, and he had agreed, to leave the hair of his chest and stomach. She did a pretty good job once she stopped acting like a fool, he thought, especially in knowing when to stop shaving the upper arms so the hair naturally blended with that of the lower. Overall, even Heidi had to agree, it worked.

Mike tightened his abdominal muscles and tensed his chest while pacing back and forth. He could see immediately that flexing, breathing normally, and walking like it was just another day at the pool would be no easy task. For one thing, his face was too tense from the effort. Of course, muscles that were more taut to begin with would help. He would definitely need to start working out again. There was an old set of weights in his garage and sit-ups would have to be a daily ritual.

"Still, not bad," he thought, holding his body firm while managing to relax his face. He nodded to his reflection and strode out of the bathhouse, slicing through the sunshine as the hot concrete pleasantly stung the soles of his feet. New pool. New look. New man.

The lifeguard, one of the Porter girls, gave him a smile. She couldn't have been more than eighteen, but everything was in place, supple and tender, browning in the sun. Mike smiled back and noted that he wasn't breathing. He'd have to work on that. Being looked at differently and more often was going to take some getting used to. He draped his towel over a new lawn chair and leaned into it like a man reclining into a better life.

Then Peter Silverman bounced through the gate and something very close to panic surged in the pit of Mike's strained abdomen. With his lopsided grin and eyes darting every which way, Peter looked like a comedian about to step up to the microphone, which was exactly what he had hoped to be before his father left him the town bakery and a bunch of real estate. They weren't exactly friends, but Peter had so few friends that he counted anyone who wasn't an enemy.

"I see they let just about anybody in down here," Peter shrieked from across the pool, his bald head bobbing like it was attached to his body by a spring.

"I guess so," Mike shouted back.

Peter stopped when he saw the Porter girl. He gestured toward the gate and said to her, "Hey sweetie, the Miss America pageant went that way."

"Huh?" the girl said.

"I say, the Miss America pageant went that way."

She looked in the direction he was pointing and smiled, "What?"

"The Miss America pageant. Haven't you ever heard of that?"

"Yeah, sure."

"Well, you look like you just stepped out of it." Peter looked her up and down. "Man alive, you should join up. You'd get my vote. Old PA would win for sure!"

The girl tried to smile but only appeared queasy. "Thanks," she said, and walked toward the women's bathhouse.

Peter moved in Mike's direction but kept his eyes fixed on the girl's bikinied bottom. When she stepped inside, he turned to Mike and said, as if it were somehow relevant to their lives, "She's legal, you know. We did her birthday cake at the bakery last week."

Mike didn't comment.

"Why aren't you at work?" Peter asked.

"Why aren't you?"

"Hey, I'm the boss. I can do whatever I want."

Then Peter's eyes hit Mike's hairless shoulders like two spotlights. As his usual cornball grin twisted into a quizzical one, Mike frantically attempted to distract him. "I figured this place would be too humble for you."

But it was too late.

"What did you do?" Peter smirked.

"Nothing. What are you talking about?" Mike's face was aflame. "What are you looking at?"

The Porter girl came out of the bathhouse. She was within earshot.

"Is something on me?" Mike brushed at his shoulder neurotically, knocking away some imaginary bee or mosquito. "What is it?"

"Where's all your hair?"

Mike nervously ran his fingers through his hair and said, "I got it cut last week," then snapped, "I see you're still bald."

Peter touched his scalp. "Yeah, well, when it goes, it don't usually return."

A young mother with two dark-haired little girls under five years old came to the gate and the lifeguard walked over to greet them.

Mike thought of Peter's nickname back in high school: The Jokester. Peter had loved it, which showed how out of tune he was with the rest of the world. The name was anything but a compliment. They called him that because he wasn't funny, because he tried too hard to be funny, and the only jokes that ever got any response at all were the ones that came at someone else's expense.

However, The Jokester must have picked up some intuition over the years because he backed off a bit. He surveyed the pool and said, "Yeah, I had to come down and see it for myself. They have been talking about building this thing forever. Can't believe they finally did it."

"Yeah," Mike said, relieved, more than happy to talk about the pool, to make small talk. "We really needed something around here. The kids don't have much to do when school's out."

"That's the truth. Keep the brats out of trouble, right? Of course, it'll take the township forever to pay for it."

"My kids will love it though."

"Sure." Peter pulled a new lawn chair next to Mike's and dropped down into it.

Before Peter had a chance to turn the conversation in another direction, Mike asked, "Is Karla with you?"

"Naw. I escaped. She's visiting her old lady."

"Yeah. I'm on my own today too."

Mike shifted his dollar-store sunglasses and closed his eyes to the bright sun.

"So did you have it done somewhere?" Peter said.

"What?"

"The hair on your back. What did you do, go to some beauty shop and have them yank it out?"

Mike opened his eyes. The lifeguard and young mother were still talking by the gate. The little girls splashed in the baby pool. "Hell no."

"Then what'd you do?"

Mike wanted to tell him to mind his own damn business and take the hint that he didn't want to discuss it, but instead, his voice suddenly went weak and defensive and he said, "I've always...I was just experimenting—"

"Experimenting?" Peter echoed through an out-of-control smirk. When he got on a roll of jokes, he always reminded Mike of a toy that was wound up too tight, and at that moment he looked like he was about to cut loose. "You didn't shave, did you?"

"What's it to you?"

Peter exploded into laughter. "You shaved your back?!"

The lifeguard and young mother looked over.

"Ooo boy," he scrunched up his face, "that's nasty." He was a mass of quivering twitches as Mike imagined him stepping up to an invisible microphone. "You must spend a fortune on shaving cream. Five o'clock shadows must be pure hell. No, but seriously, I mean, how do you reach it? Isn't it itchy?"

Mike was trapped. He thought about grabbing the wiry little pinhead by the neck, but was afraid of the damage he might do to him. So he did the only thing he could do. He laid back, closed his eyes and ignored him.

"What, you're not talking now?"

Mike took off his sunglasses and said through clenched teeth, "If you don't shut your big, stupid, ugly mouth, I'm going to shut it for you."

Peter looked like a kid who'd had his lollipop ripped away from him for no reason at all. "What the hell kind of way is that to talk?"

"Look. Do you mind staying out of my personal business?"

Peter got to his feet. "Not at all," he said, and stammered around for a better exit line. "I'll tell you what, though. You're the one who…you are supposed to be at work. You're rude as hell."

Mike laid back. He pretended to close his eyes but still watched Peter through his eyelashes. The Jokester had no more talent at delivering exit lines than he had at being funny, yet true to himself, he refused to accept that. He stood there for another moment, muttered, "I'll tell you. Some people…" and walked to the other end of the pool, slapping his feet scornfully on the concrete.

It was a relief to be rid of Peter, but it wasn't easy to shake his feelings of guilt and impending doom. His guilt was a direct result of the look on Peter's face before he stormed off. It was the same pitiful expression Peter wore most of the way through high school when no one laughed at his jokes or when all of the boys, even the ones on his own team, ganged up on him in Dodge Ball. It was the baffled stare of an awkward kid who had forgotten for a moment and was then reminded that no one liked him.

The impending doom came from the knowledge that Peter would tell anyone who would listen about the incident and how it had all started because of a shaved back. For a moment, he thought about going over to him and apologizing, saying that he just wasn't himself. Possibly making up a good lie about the hair on his back. Maybe chemotherapy. Saying that it didn't affect all of his hair, just some of it.

He knew it would never work and decided he'd wasted enough thought on Peter. He was going to enjoy the day. Tomorrow it would be back to the fluorescent lights and monotony of Lyndora Business Forms, but today, the sun felt good and the water sparkled. The Porter girl had climbed up into the tall lifeguard stand next to the water. Her legs were long, tan, and smooth dangling from the chair. She swung them playfully back and fourth. The effect on Mike was hypnotic and he drifted off to sleep.

Four days had passed since Mike last shaved.

It was 3:30 in the morning and he sat on the porch sipping a tall glass of vodka and orange juice and ice. Sleeping was impossible when one was covered in little black hairs. The itching was maddening, but the drink put a nice burn in his chest and he enjoyed the clinking of ice every time he raised the glass.

Heidi was right, of course. It was ridiculous. To maintain it, he had to shave every day, and it seemed to take forever. Heidi was even less thrilled than he was about having one extra task every morning before work. She was good about it though. She knew that he realized his mistake. He alone made the decision to stop the craziness and let it grow back. She also must have told Jerry and Jenny not to mention it to Daddy anymore because he hadn't heard a word from them about it for two days.

Mike scratched the wild, irritable hairs covering his back with a long kitchen spoon and looked at the sky. A dark cloud moved across the full moon and he felt that his life was an unending series of mean cycles. Once again, he had taken action only to find that it was the wrong action, made a bold move only to have it come back and bite him in the ass—the hairy ass. Five years ago, after hitting thirty, he had rolled up his sleeves and taken drastic measures. He bought books by Zig Ziglar and Norman Vincent Peale. He made plans and set goals. He picked up a side job selling heavy-duty cleaning products, bought an old Honda motorcycle that needed some work, and built a new porch on the house. He even had Heidi write out a wish list and helped her revise it. (Her first draft suffered from "small thinking" and contained things like breakfast in bed and a weekend in the mountains.)

But even then, when he was going great guns quoting Ziglar and Peale like a preacher dropping scripture, he had to admit that, deep in his brain, he feared that his greatness would never come to pass. That, among other things, Heidi's wish list would go unfulfilled. That the whole exercise was just part of a big, cruel cycle.

And now, tonight, here he was at thirty-five, sitting on his crooked porch and looking at the Honda still sitting in the yard, silhouetted against the night sky. It still needed work. He walked over to it, climbed on, and wrapped his hands around the padded handlebars. The springs creaked under his weight.

Nope. He couldn't even imagine riding it anymore. Someone rode it, though. Someone rode the life out of it and pawned it off on a soap salesman. A sucker with a hairy back. He looked at the house. With the uneven porch, the house looked like it had a harelip.

"Sorry, house," he said, "I didn't mean to drag you down with me."

Mike was lonely for the warmth in his chest and the clink of the ice. As he crawled off the bike, his stomach muscles ached from the sit-ups he'd been doing. He hadn't done them for four days now. Surprise, surprise. He slapped his stomach as he made his way to the porch. Let 'er hang, he thought.

If he were a woman or a different kind of man, he would have had a good cry. Heidi did that from time to time after a bad day at work or even an argument. He always told her not to cry, that things weren't so bad, and she'd tell him she wanted to because it made her feel better. And she always did seem better afterwards. Lighter somehow.

Mike imagined himself letting everything drain out in big, sloppy sobs. It would be a ludicrous sight, but the relief would be good. He gave it a try, starting with a few quick sighs, then widening his eyes. He even rubbed his fingers in them, but it was no use. He just wasn't a crier. Never had been.

He finished his drink. After the clinking of the ice, he noticed there was no sound. He listened hard. Surely there must be a distant car or plane somewhere. But he heard nothing. He closed his eyes. It was like the world had stopped churning and gathered into a quiet pool so he could rethink everything. Or maybe so he could stop thinking and just be there and hold the silence.

So he did. For a long while, he did. When he opened his eyes, he realized that even without the benefit of crying, he felt a good bit better. It was refreshing to be awake when the rest of the world was asleep.

There wasn't much of the night left, but he was going to ride it out and watch the sun come up. Then, for the hell of it, he was going to surprise Heidi with breakfast in bed. And if she was game, they were only a few hours from some pretty nice mountains.

Then it struck him that God had quite a sense of humor. All night he'd been sitting there, under the full moon, with hair sprouting out all over his body, and he had completely missed the joke. He laughed out loud and unleashed a long howl that came from the bottom of his toes and went all the way to the moon.

A DANG SHAME

It was a dang shame about his hair.

That's exactly what I told the cops when they came around asking what I knew about Dean Smith. They looked at me like I was nuts, not that I care. Everyone knows that Dean caused quite a stir in town the other day, but not many people take the time to think about what drove him to do the things he did. Well, I'll tell you, a tender heart and a sorry head of hair is a bad combination.

Dean's hair started receding when he was only sixteen or seventeen. Made his forehead look terrible big, but he could have handled that. The worst part was the color and the look of it: bright orange and all kinky, like balls of wire. And there was not a thing he could do about it. No way to make it look nice. Poor fella tried everything. No matter what he did, he was always the quiet kid with the loud hair. High school was a tough row to hoe because of it. Everyone either picked on him or ignored him.

Working in the high school cafeteria every day, I see and hear plenty. Course, I knew Dean from little up. Lived just across the street. He didn't have brothers or sisters, but he wasn't the least bit spoiled. He was about twelve when my man died and I hired him to mow the grass and keep my flower bed weeded. I couldn't afford to pay much and figured he'd want to get out of it when he got into his teens. You know how snooty most teenagers are.

Not Dean, though. He always smiled and spoke to me when he went through the lunch line and mowed my lawn clean up until he graduated high school. Good worker, too. I never once had to harp at him about anything.

Most of the fighting and all of the heavy drinking didn't start until his senior year. Before all that, there was only one group of girls that was nice to him. They were in the marching band. A far cry from the cheerleader crowd, but I'm sure he was happy to have some girls to flirt with anyway. I'd see them carrying on at the library in town from time to time. Gwen Anderson was part of that group. You could see right away that she liked him. His hair didn't seem to bother her a bit. Course, she was overweight. Pretty face, but terrible big for a young girl.

When it came time for senior pictures, Dean was very self-conscious about it. So the girls in the band set out to help him. Now I don't know whose idea it was and I'm pretty sure it wasn't Gwen's, but one of that bunch got the bright idea to straighten and color his hair. At any rate, Dean went along with it. Well, what a mistake. They sure didn't know what they were doing because it came out an awful shade of brown, very unnatural looking and so brittle that you swore it'd just crumble off in your fingers if you touched it.

My, oh my, did the kids torture him over that one. After years of being called Wire Head and Mr. Brillo, they started calling him Beauty Shop Boy. That's when the real fighting started. He'd had some scraps with the Gutterson kid every now and again, but up until that point, I knew Dean didn't like to fight and stayed away from it when he could.

I swear I witnessed the turning point. It was in the lunch line. Not uncommon. The cafeteria sees a lot of trouble, all those kids in one space. I remember we were having sloppy joes. I handed Dean his plate and asked him how his mom and dad were. He smiled nice and said they were fine. Then, old Gutterson, they call him Chopper, I don't know why, came up next to Dean. It was no coincidence that they were next to each other in line. Gutterson planned it, I'm sure. He shoved Dean aside to get to the ketchup and called him Beauty Shop Boy. Well, I'd seen Dean endure a heck of a lot worse than that, but for whatever reason, that was the brick that broke the load. Dean, very calmly, set down his tray and whammed Chopper right smack in the face. Now, that Chopper does a lot of fighting, but he went straight down, and Dean just picked up his tray and walked away. Someone started clapping and then a bunch of kids joined in. A couple teachers came in then and got Gutterson to his feet. I'm telling you I never saw a kid so stunned. Blood was just pouring out of his mouth and his front tooth was in the palm of his hand.

Gutterson was sent to the nurse's office and Dean to see the principal. As soon as we got the rest of the kids through the line, I went to the front office and told old Kavanaugh that I saw the whole thing and Gutterson was asking for what he got. Well, it didn't do a bit of good. He said that those boys had a history of fighting that went back to the ninth grade and he would continue to punish them both equally until they graduated or stopped fighting, whichever came first.

Kids started taking Dean more seriously after that one, and don't think he didn't notice it either. They still made fun of his hair, but not so much to his face anymore. That's when the McGowan girl started to take notice of him. Now, she's a story and a half. Had a kid to God only knows who before she was a junior in high school. Course her parents ended up taking care of it most of the time. Then she got together with Gutterson and they were quite an item: lovey-dovey one minute and fighting the next. Well, they were fighting when Gutterson lost his tooth and she must have wanted to rub salt in the wound by going after Dean. It made Gutterson mad alright, but it was poor old Dean that got the short end of the stick.

That McGowan girl was a low-life and a you-know-what but she no sooner set her sights on Dean than she had him. He went head over heels for her, probably thought his luck was changing for the better. But if you ask me, aside from being born with a hideous head of hair, that was the worst thing that ever happened to him.

For one thing, it completely killed any chance he might have had of getting together with Gwen. She was more suited to him in every way. They were both decent kids and could have made a good life for themselves. They matched each other. In the looks department, they each had their cross to bear with her being heavy and him having that hair. It put them at the same level of attractiveness. That's the way life works best. A person rarely clicks with someone better or worse looking than they are. But I guess Dean wanted more for himself and thought he finally had his chance when the McGowan girl came along. I hate to say it, but it was no mystery why she turned heads. She was a pretty thing in high school. Course that type goes downhill fast and a young fellow never thinks to take that into account when he's smitten.

Her no-good crowd had a terrible effect on Dean. All they did was drink and smoke dope. Pretty soon old Dean didn't have time for the girls in the marching band anymore. He started growing his hair long and wild. For heaven's sake, what a sight that was. It grew *out* instead of down and looked like a giant, orange ball sitting on top of his shoulders.

McGowan never cared about him. Gave him nothing but heartache. He was just a safe bet, that's all. Every time you turned around she was mad at him about something and giving back his class ring. A bunch of bull crap is all that was. She picked fights with him so she had an excuse to lay around with other bums. That's what they were too: bums. Some of them were in their twenties and thirties and more than one of them were married. She pulled that on him right before the senior prom so she could go with some fellow from Butler with a fancy convertible.

So Dean didn't go at all. He'd already been fitted for his tux and everything, but he didn't want to go alone and didn't figure he could get anyone else to go with him. He showed up after school to mow my lawn. "For goodness' sake, Dean," I said. "Get out of here. It's prom night."

But his mind was made up. He acted like he didn't care and was as polite and nice to me as ever. I can still see him out there pushing the mower around the yard, sweating in the heat. His face looked so tiny in that mass of crazy hair. Every time our eyes met, he'd smile at me.

Later that night, he hooked up with a couple from her crowd and they started drinking. I've heard people say that there's happy drinkers and sad ones. Well, Dean was a mad one. When he was drinking, he was extra sensitive to being made fun of and those were the only times I ever knew him to go looking for trouble. He was certainly looking for it when they crashed the prom.

Dean tried talking to McGowan and of course the fellow with the convertible wasn't going to just stand by. He took one look at Dean and burst into laughter. Dean's nose turned red when he was drinking heavy and with that bush of hair it didn't take much imagination to see a clown. McGowan's date started calling him Bozo and two seconds later they were on the floor. When the cops came, they hauled Dean off and charged him with underage drinking and a pile of other things. His so-called friends were long gone by the time the cops got there.

Old McGowan loved the attention and no one can tell me any different. A week later, she made up with Dean. The Bozo remark must have stuck with her though, because she insisted that he change his hair. He never argued with her. She was the reason it was long in the first place. She must have had the idea that he'd look more rugged if he buzzed most of it off, but she was wrong. He was too thin; his neck was too long. Besides, there was nothing tough about a head covered with orange fuzz.

After graduation, his drinking got heavier than ever. That's about the time McGowan started up with Gutterson again. She wanted to keep it a big secret. Everyone knew, though. She wasn't out of high school two months and she was pregnant again. Dean surely must have known there was a good chance it wasn't his, but instead of telling that old rip to hit the road, he went in the other direction and asked her to marry him. Desperate is all I can figure. He must have thought being married would change her. My, oh my, young people do the stupidest things. She said yes, of course, and they set the date a year in advance because she didn't want to look fat in her wedding dress. I'm sure she didn't have the slightest intention of being faithful. Knowing her, she probably just wanted to be queen for a day. I honestly think that's all the further a number of girls think it through.

They had the ceremony in the Protestant church in town. Anything goes in that church, I guess. She wore white. Her kids were at the wedding. The baby, and believe me, I wasn't the only one to notice, was the spitting image of Gutterson.

Dean rented a white tuxedo and would have looked real handsome if it weren't for the hair. It was back to orange wire and receding terrible. That marriage would have never happened if he'd have been born with better hair. Everything would have been different. People would have really looked at him then and seen his kindness. His good nature. I'd bet anything he'd have had a great sense of humor too, but no one is going to laugh *with* you when they are busy laughing *at* you. Or feeling sorry for you.

The girls, the pretty ones, really missed out because they never even considered him. Dean was the big loser, though. Course he wasn't without blame when it came to judging people by looks. Gwen was a good example of that. She went off to college somewhere and never did come back around here. He'd have been a lot happier with her, there's no doubt, but that thing he married was definitely prettier at the time.

They were only married about six months before the night of the incident. He was drinking heavy at that point. Everyone knows that.

Gutterson had been messing around with Dean's wife when Dean was at work. They thought they were real clever, but no one was fooled. He'd park his truck in front of the Ruffled Grouse. She'd dump the kids off with her parents and pick him up out back in her car. Then they'd disappear. I heard they went to the Clarion Cozy Inn sometimes and other times they just drove out into the woods or into the strip cuts.

Anyway, Dean left work at lunchtime that day and stopped at the Ruffled Grouse when he saw Gutterson's pick-up. They say Dean sat at the bar for a couple of hours drinking one after the other. He kept asking why Chopper wasn't around if his truck was out there. No one gave him an honest answer even though they all knew. Dean knew it too, that's why he'd left work early in the first place and it was why he kept drinking and asking.

After a while, he stumbled out to his car. He took a ball bat out of the trunk and started beating on Gutterson's fancy pick-up like there was no tomorrow. Some people said he was laughing, others said he was crying. Either way, it was a pitiful sight. He was completely out of control. No one tried to stop him, though the bartender threatened to call the cops and finally did. They say Dean just hammered and pounded on that truck for everything that was wrong in the world. There wasn't a piece of glass intact or a smooth piece of metal when he finally put that bat down.

When he saw the cops coming, he climbed into his car and took off. They chased him of course, sirens screaming and the whole bit. Even though he was drunk, it's pretty much common knowledge that he drove his car into the tree on purpose. I don't like to say that because only God knows the truth, and considering what the Bible says about taking your own life, I sure hope it was an accident. I'd like to think that Dean has some peace in the next world. Sure never had any here. But the good Lord can see beyond hair.

Anyway, now his hog of a wife can run around with Gutterson all she wants to. They both have a lot to think about, though I doubt they will. I can't bring myself to speak to either one. When I see them out, I go the other way. Maybe that's not right, but I just can't help it.

I have Dean's senior picture on my wall. He ended up wearing a ball cap for it. His smile wasn't natural and you could tell it was a put-on. Still, I have to say, he looked nice and really did have a handsome face. But no one noticed. All they saw was the hair.

What a shame. What a dang shame.

DREAMS

"Over time," a doctor warned Ernie years ago, "the monotonous rhythm of that machine will draw the life right out of your body."

A guy didn't need to be a doctor to figure that one out, Ernie thought. He knew all about the pain and numbness that came from the repetitive motions of running the press at Lyndora Business Forms. For Ernie, the pain was in his lower back, the numbness in his arms. It made him feel older than his almost fifty years, and he wondered if he'd ever have a good night's sleep again.

He was on the evening shift this week and was preparing for an order of 500,000 credit card statements.

"Ernie boy!" Howard shouted.

"Yeah?" Ernie said, rinsing the photo plate with water from a hose.

"It's your turn to take the new kid tonight," Howard said, patting his beer belly. "I did it last night. I'm not paid to be a damned baby-sitter."

"I'll take him," Ernie said. "What's he like?"

"Weird."

"So he'll fit right in, huh?"

"Yeah, right," Howard said and belched. "Onions. Damn."

"What's weird about him?"

Howard shrugged his shoulders. "He's a skinny little shit. Asks too many questions. Always writing in a little note pad."

"Maybe he's a spy," Ernie said.

"Yeah. I wouldn't put it past the tight-asses upstairs," Howard said, nodding at the row of mirrored office windows above them.

"Since when can they afford to do any hiring?"

"Since they can get dumb-ass kids to work for damn near nothing."

"Get enough of those, they won't need us anymore."

"That's the plan, Ernie boy," Howard said, and walked away. Then he shouted over his shoulder, "But they expect us to train the little bastards."

Ernie had the press ready to go except for the inking, which was always a bitch on a multicolored print, when the kid came over. "Are you Ernie?" the kid asked.

"Yep."

"I think I'm working with you tonight," he said, and held out his hand. Ernie shook it. The kid looked him square in the eye, squeezing his knuckles as he pumped his hand. "I'm Seth Hardy."

"You're going to be a packer tonight."

"Fine with me."

"Is that what Howard had you doing last night?"

"No. He had me scrubbing stains off the floor and cleaning the glue out of the binding machine."

Ernie chuckled.

Seth looked around and added, "I don't think he likes me too much."

"Don't take it personally," Ernie said, going back to the press. "Howard's alright, but he takes some getting used to."

"What do you need me to do?"

"Nothing."

"Nothing?"

"Well, not yet, anyway. You can't start packing until I get the machine fired up, and what I'm doing is a one-man job."

Seth stood in silence for a minute or two. "Do you mind if I walk around?"

"Don't matter to me," he said. "But you're part-time, ain't you?"

"Yeah."

"Well, if you want a full-time job you'd better look busy. Grab a broom and sweep the floor."

Seth looked at the floor. "It's clean as a pin."

Ernie said, "That's because all the part-timers want to be full-timers. Got to look busy even if you're not. It's all about putting on a good show for the big boys upstairs."

"I'm not too interested in full-time," Seth said. He put his hands in his pockets. "If it's okay with you, I'd like to walk around a little until you're ready."

"Don't matter to me," Ernie said. "Just be within earshot when I fire this thing up."

"Thanks."

Seth pulled a small blue note pad and pen out of his pocket and took notes as he walked around. This was his second day of work. He was eager to really look at the place since he had no intention of being around long enough to get sick of it. It was laid out like a huge warehouse. There were forty large green and gray printing presses. Stations, they called them.

Each one had a yellow sign with a black number bolted onto it. The machines were long, with dozens of rollers and hundreds of knobs and gauges and colored lights. The place had a smell, too. The pungent smell of ink and new paper.

At the back of the presses, there were computer screens where the main printers, guys like Ernie and Howard, spent a lot of time before actually turning on the machines. This was also where giant rolls of paper, five feet wide and four feet high, stood on end.

Ernie came to the back of the press and sat on the stool next to the computer.

"How do they get that roll of paper into the press?" Seth wanted to know.

"Forklift," Ernie mumbled, staring at the computer screen.

Seth wrote that down. He also described Ernie as a small man with dark hair, gold-rimmed glasses, a weary voice, and a pockmarked face. He added that Ernie was an older guy who seemed dull, but was friendly enough. Then Seth walked on to the next station, where he saw Howard picking his nose.

"What the hell are you looking at?" Howard asked.

"Nothing," Seth said, and when he was far enough away, he wrote, "Howard is an asshole."

There was a stockroom about half the size of a football field with giant rolls of paper stacked twenty feet high. And next to that was a trash room with dozens of bins overflowing with paper.

"What are you doing?" some guy in dress clothes and a tie asked Seth.

Seth stuck his pad and pen in his pocket and said, "I'm working with Ernie. He's not quite ready for me yet, so—"

"Grab a broom," he said. "You're not being paid to stand around."

"Where's one at?"

He pointed to the corner. "Wake up! There are brooms everywhere around here." The guy put his hands on his hips and looked disgusted. "What's your name?"

"Seth Hardy."

The guy nodded, like he was going to remember that name if anything went wrong.

Seth continued to walk around looking at the place, letting the broom glide across the floor in front of him. He watched the guy with the tie take the black metal stairs up to the offices at the far end of the plant. Seth made a mental note of the mirrored windows to put into his notebook later on. After he'd covered the area, he started working his way back to Ernie's station. As he passed the trash room he heard a commotion. Inside, a low-lift held a pallet full of packaged boxes. A round, bald man was slicing them open and dumping them into the trash bins.

"You new?" the guy said.

"Yeah."

He pointed to the broom. "I can tell by your third arm there."

"I'm Seth," he said, and stuck out his hand.

The round man glanced at the office windows upstairs and nodded without stopping his work. "Brian. Everyone calls me Shorty."

"Why are you dumping those?"

The round man tore open a fresh box and took a single bank statement from it. He pointed to the bank logo at the top of the page. "Right there." The logo had the tiniest smudge. "Some dizzy bastard ran a million, one million copies, without noticing it. Packed them up, sent them out, and Mellon Bank sent them right back."

"So you have to do them over? All of them?"

"I don't, but somebody does. Every last one. You've got to have a good eye for this kind of work. The printing part, anyway. A lot of these guys are getting up there: fifties, sixties. I'm not mentioning any names, but some of these guys better watch their step."

"What happened to the guy who messed this one up?"

"Gone. Has a wife and three kids, too."

"Wow."

"That's life without a union. Called him upstairs at lunchtime, and that afternoon a broom-pusher was promoted to printer."

Seth looked at the broom in his hands. "That's tough."

The round man glanced around and said in a low voice, "That broom-pusher just happened to be a nephew of one of the big boys. Definitely pre-trained. Waiting for the older guy to fuck up."

"You really think so?"

"Hell yeah. You don't just walk into a printing job. That's pretty technical shit." He smacked his chubby hands together. "This kid waltzes right in and takes over. And another thing," he said, squinting his eyes. "Why didn't anyone else, the guys on the next shift, for example, notice the smudge? A million copies takes a long, long time to print."

Seth looked at the round man and shook his head very slowly. "I'm just trying to make a little money for school," he said. "I'm not interested in full-time."

"Well, now, I couldn't blame you if you were. It's a shame, that's all. The working man's got no rights anymore." Then he looked over Seth's shoulder and mumbled, "You better get moving."

The guy with the tie was standing in the corner, arms folded, staring at him. Seth started pushing the broom again and worked his way back to Ernie's station.

Ernie winked at him. "I was just about to holler for you. We're ready."

Howard shouted from his press, "Hey, Ernie boy! Better watch that kid. I hear he likes to FTD!"

Seth asked Ernie what FTD meant. Ernie smiled and turned the press on. It made a screeching sound and a deep roar as the paper rolled through the machine. Then it settled into a rhythm: clap, clack, clap, clack, clap, clack.

"Fuck the dog," Ernie shouted.

"Huh?"

"FTD," Ernie's voice strained over the machine, "is fucking the dog."

Seth stared at him.

"Fucking the dog means goofing off. Not working."

"Ohhhh," Seth nodded his head.

Seth stood on one side of the press and Ernie stood on the other. A stack of credit card forms began creeping out of the mouth of the machine. Ernie said loudly, "There's fluorescent lighting under here. When the machine has printed one box-full, you'll see a dab of ink that shows only under the light." He pointed to it on the accordion-like stack, which was creeping across the press in front of them. "You cut it here," which he did, using a razor blade that was taped to a wooden handle. "Then flip the stack on its end," which he did also.

Then he showed Seth how to quickly fold a box, check the top and bottom forms for mistakes, pack the forms into the box, seal it, stamp it, and stack it on a wooden pallet. When that was done, it was time to cut another stack to be boxed up. "We've both got to keep moving at a good pace," Ernie said, "or we'll get backed up. Once we start the machine, we're not supposed to stop it unless there is a mistake in the printing or the job is done."

After Seth completed his first box, he said, "This isn't too bad."

"I guess," Ernie said. "Might feel different at the end of the day, though. This is what we'll be doing for the next seven hours."

"What about lunch?"

"We don't punch out for lunch, so we don't technically have a lunch break. But I can slow the press down so one of us can pack while the other one eats."

So it was cut, stack, fold, check, check, pack, seal, stamp, and stack. Neither of them said anything until Seth sneezed four times in a row.

"Damn," he said.

"It's the dust," Ernie said. "Covers everything. It's too fine to see, or even feel, but it's there. When you get outside you'll smell it on your skin and your clothes. Sometimes you even taste it. But you get used to it."

"Been here long?" Seth asked.

"Since the place opened. Fourteen years."

"Like it?"

Ernie shrugged his shoulders. Did he like it? It had been years since he'd thought about it, if he'd ever thought about it at all. It was a job. Everyone needed a job. "I've done worse for less money."

"Do printers make good money?"

"Not bad. Good for the area. The benefits are the thing: hospitalization, sick days, life insurance."

"Seems decent."

"I guess. I had to put in a lot of years to get them, though. And there's no guarantees. One screw-up and they can take it all back."

There was just the roar of the machine for a long time.

Ernie felt like there was a butcher knife wedged into his lower back. His arms were tingling. To take his mind off it, he said, "What were you writing in that little book a while ago?"

"Just taking notes on the place. I'm a writer."

"Really?" Ernie had never met a writer before. "You've written books?"

"Not published, yet. I write short stories. Publishing takes time. It's a tough business to get into. I'm studying literature at Butler Community College."

"Is that a good school?"

"I guess. They only offer one creative writing course, though. I'm taking it this semester. It'll have to do until I can save the money to go to a bigger school."

"What kind of stories do you write?"

"No particular kind. My teacher says to write what you know, so they're mostly about living around here. Not too exciting. My favorites are Jack London and Ernest Hemingway, but I need to see the world before I can write like them."

"You should write scary ones. Like Stephen King. He makes millions."

"Yeah, I like some of his books. Which ones have you read?"

"I'm not much of a reader, but I've seen his movies. They're scary. Some of them."

"I'll think about it."

"So, you're writing about this place?"

"Maybe. I always write stories about where I work."

"This place is scary," Ernie smiled. Once his arms were tingling, he knew a screaming headache would soon follow. Like clockwork, he thought. "How often do you write?"

"Anytime I can. That's why I don't want to work full-time."

"So you're telling me I may be working with a famous writer, huh?"

"Someday." Seth knew that a lot of people made fun of his goals, so he set them straight right away when they asked. "I don't care how hard it is. The way I figure it, if you hang in there long enough, you can make anything happen."

Ernie half spoke, half sang in a dry, cracking voice, "Chasing the big dream..."

"Is that a song?"

"Sure! Don't you listen to country music?"

"Not a lot."

"That's my old lady's favorite country band: The Roadies."

"Don't think I've ever heard of them. You like country music?"

"I like all kinds of music. Except the new rock and roll. It's just a lot of noise, if you ask me. The old rock and roll, the fifties stuff, now that I like." Ernie stamped a box and said, "Anyway, remember me when you hit the big time."

Ernie looked at the kid and wondered what it would be like if he really did make it, instead of ending up like everyone else he knew. "Where you from?"

"Cherry Run."

"Pretty up that way. I used to hunt up there."

Fourteen years. The thought pounded in Ernie's temples. He couldn't figure out where it all went. It was like he turned around and he was thirty and then he was forty and next week, he'd be fifty. Half a century. Things just kept rolling on toward the end. Just like the clap, clack, clap, clack of the press.

Ernie knew this kid didn't have a bad back and numb arms and a throbbing head. This kid, this Seth, really believed he was going to be a big writer. And that made Ernie feel hopeful and hopeless at the same time. He wanted to tell the kid to go for it, as they say. He wanted to tell him to save his money and get the hell out of here. Go someplace like California or New York and make it big.

And yet, he wanted to tell the kid that everyone has dreams and that most people's don't come true. He wanted to tell him not to take it so hard if he never made it as a writer, because it's a big dream. When you're from a place like Cherry Run or Rimersburg or Sligo or even Butler, it's pretty near impossible to have a big dream come true.

Of course, there was Jim Kelly. He was from East Brady and he went all the way to quarterback for the Buffalo Bills. That's as big as big time gets. But football's more popular than writing, Ernie thought. Everyone watches football, not a lot of people read books.

Howard came over and plopped himself down on a folding chair. He took off a sock and shoe.

"What the hell are you doing?" Ernie asked him.

"Fucking the dog," Howard groaned and stared at his bare foot. "Damn press is down again. Got some so-called mechanic screwing with it."

"I mean with your foot."

"Got a corn." Howard took out a pocket knife and began to cut into his foot. "Cutting off the dead skin makes it feel better."

"Seth here goes to Butler Community College."

Howard didn't say anything.

"Howard's boy goes there."

"Yeah, he wants to transfer to Pitt next year," Howard said.

"I'd do that if I had the money," Seth said. "I used to know a girl who went to Pitt. She liked it."

"I'd like it myself," Howard said. "There's more pussy down there than a guy knows what to do with."

"You wouldn't know what to do with it anyway," Ernie said.

Howard sliced off a chunk of skin from his foot and threw it at Ernie. "You can pick that up and have it with your lunch later," he said to Seth.

Seth didn't answer.

"Lighten up, kid. I'm just fooling with you." Then Howard walked away without putting his shoe and sock back on.

"Howard's a strange bird," Ernie said.

Seth grumbled, "Seems like an asshole to me."

"Well, he takes getting used to," Ernie said. "Maybe you could write a story about him. Make him a mass murderer. A guy about to explode."

"Nah. I don't want to write a story about him."

"Well, whatever you do, don't write one about me," Ernie said.

"Why?"

"Put people to sleep. Be a pretty boring story." Then he said, "It would be funny to read about yourself in a book, though. Even if it was boring."

Seth became aware of the note pad in his pocket and the description it contained of Ernie. It wasn't a very flattering one. He wondered what Ernie would say if he knew he'd described him as dull and noted the pockmarks on his face.

"Do you ever write your dreams?" Ernie said. "You know, the kind of dreams you have at night when you're sleeping?"

"No. Mine never make sense. They make sense while I'm asleep, but when I wake up, they're just a bunch of jumbled images."

Ernie nodded. As he sealed up another box, he said, "I have a dream you could write. It would be funny. I've had the dream for almost twenty years now."

"The same one?"

"Yep. I must have had it ten, fifteen times in the last twenty years. It's always the same."

"Tell me."

Ernie snickered at himself and shook his head. He had never told anyone about the dream before. Once, he started to tell his wife, but she thought it was so silly that she wasn't even interested in hearing the whole thing. "It's funny," Ernie said again. "It would make a funny story, but that's all it would be good for. A joke story. Do you like Frank Sinatra?"

"Not really," Seth said, "but I guess he used to be a big deal."

"Oh, yeah. For sure. Anyway, I always liked his music. I don't know why. There was just something about it."

"Uh huh," Seth said, thinking Ernie might stop any minute without the encouragement.

"Well, in the dream, I'm dressed in a black tuxedo. Ruffles, tails, the whole bit. And I'm on stage in some big place. Like one of those opera houses in New York, or a giant theater or something, and—" he shook his head, "and I'm singing this Frank Sinatra song. I don't know which one, but in the dream I know it well and everyone in the audience knows it." He stopped packing and held his arms out in front of himself as he talked, sort of reaching at the air. "And I sound great. I mean, better than Frank." His eyes were wide, amazed, behind the gold-rimmed glasses. "My voice is perfect. It's big and full. Everyone is in awe of me. They're just staring, you know? And I'm in awe of myself. It just sounds so good, and it's coming out of me like nothing."

Ernie looked right at Seth. Seth stopped working too.

"It's the strangest thing," Ernie said. "I'm actually disappointed when I first wake up. But the dream is easy to remember and the feeling of it stays with me. I'm in a great mood all day after that dream."

Ernie looked at the forms, which were about to drop off the end of the press. "Son of a bitch!" he said. "Just cut and stack them on the floor till we get caught up. We'll box them later."

They worked fast, and fifteen minutes later things were back to normal again.

"Maybe you should be a singer," Seth said.

"Huh?"

"Maybe that's what the dream means. Maybe it means you should be a singer."

"Yeah, right. I'll get started on that as soon as I hit the lottery."

"No, I mean it."

"Me, a singer. That's a good one."

"Wouldn't you like it?"

"Sure, but what's that got to do with it?"

"If you'd like it, you should try it."

Ernie watched him closely to see if the kid was making fun of him. But Seth was serious.

"It's too late," Ernie said.

"It's never too late," Seth said. "If you want something in life, you have to go get it."

For a moment, Ernie wished he hadn't told the dream. He didn't do a good enough job of explaining it anyway, and now he had gotten this kid started. "It was just a dream."

"Yeah, but you've been having it for twenty years." Seth was fired up. "Why don't you get some training?"

The pain in Ernie's back was shooting down his left leg now. "It's too late for me."

"It's never too late. I could see if they have any beginning classes at school for returning adults."

All this talk might have made him mad if Seth wasn't looking at him the way he was. The kid's eyes were shining, and he believed that what he was saying was the simplest thing. Ernie could have told Seth a lot. True things about life and the world they lived in. But they were also hard things, and this kid would have to wake up to them soon enough.

They were quiet for a while. Clap, clack, clap, clack, clap, clack. Ernie turned the speed of the press down and said, "You can eat first if you want."

"Thanks." Seth sat on a stool and took a sandwich out of his lunch bag. He opened and closed a red, irritated hand in front of him. "My hands are stinging," he said.

"Paper cuts from the forms and the boxes," Ernie said. "Plus the material is drying them out." His own hands felt like that once, a long time ago, but now they were covered with a hard, thick skin. They had adjusted to the job, and he was sure, eventually, this kid's hands would change as well.

They would have to.

TEMPORARY PEOPLE

Down in Butler, United Computer Systems had a huge order of surveys to be checked, so they hired a few temporary people to come in during the evenings to clean them up. Tim Weaver was one of them. The pay wasn't bad, and until someplace hired him full-time, it was as good as anything else. On his first day, the security guard greeted him with a blank look and methodically paged Johnny, the man in charge of the temporary people.

Johnny was a forty-something, skinny fellow wearing a sports jacket over a tie-dyed tee shirt. "Walk this way," he said to Tim, and began flapping his arms and walking like a chicken. Tim stood very still. Johnny burst into laughter and slapped him on the shoulder. "Just joshing you, kid," he said. "Come on."

The place was a maze of cubicles that served as offices. Each cubicle contained a work area with a swivel chair and a large-screened computer.

Johnny explained that Tim's shift would go from 4:00 in the afternoon until midnight. The full-time people, who did the important computer stuff, would be around until 5:30 or 6:00, during which time the place would be buzzing with the clicking of keyboards and snippets of conversation. Johnny introduced Tim to the two other temporary people, a couple of sorry-looking souls whose names Tim immediately forgot, and told them that after 6:00, they would be the only ones in the building.

"Unfortunately," Johnny said, "they have the four of us scattered all over the place, so we won't even be able to talk to each other." That was okay with Tim. He wasn't much of a talker anyway.

Tim's workstation was Cubicle 160. "Look around," Johnny said. "Pay attention to where you are in relation to everything or else you'll always be lost." At the computer, Johnny showed him how to check the surveys. Tim's job was to correctly type in anything that the computer misread.

"There's one part of the survey that's handwritten," Johnny explained. "Customer opinions. The computer is supposed to read it, but it almost never does. Expect to correct that part every time. There's twenty surveys to a batch, twenty thousand total. When you're done checking one, go to the next batch. The real challenge is staying awake." He laughed and said if they needed him, he was Cubicle 724.

It was that evening that Tim had his first encounter with Monica. She was a full-timer and her cubicle shared a wall with his. He heard her saying good-bye to a co-worker at 6:00, and for the rest of the night he couldn't get her out of his mind. Even though he'd not seen her, he knew she was beautiful. Her voice was light and fun and had a playful sexiness about it. Immediately, he wanted to see what she looked like, but the place was a massive maze to him and he had no justifiable reason to leave his computer. However, there was no rush. The idea of Monica was awakened in him, and the anticipation was nice.

By the end of his second week, Tim had acquired a great respect for Monica. Every day, between the lively hours of 4:00 and 6:00, he heard her talk about forecast meetings and cost-effectiveness. She verified data and attended conferences. She was an asset to the company and was popular with her colleagues. People were constantly stopping by to discuss this or that, and sometimes just to chat with her.

He'd still not seen her, and she knew nothing of his existence, yet he had notions of all the people she could be. She was no-nonsense. Flirtatious. Serious, but carefree. She liked to laugh. And once she was even angry. She whispered harshly to a co-worker. Tim leaned close to the carpeted wall to hear what she was saying. With sharp, clipped words, she said her supervisor was an asshole.

Tim knew that all she needed was a little positive reinforcement. The supervisor had upset her so much that she stayed late a couple of nights, doing extra work just to prove herself. Tim hated for her to have to work so hard, but he did enjoy their time together. He heard her fingers moving over the computer keyboard, and heard her sighs of exhaustion. Long, soft sighs. She picked up the phone and tapped out a number. "Hi," she said. "I'm still at work. Looks like you get home first tonight."

It was foolish for Tim to be jealous. It wasn't like he didn't know about her husband. However, she hadn't talked about him all that often, for being a newlywed. Tim felt sure that wedlock was not what Monica had hoped it would be. She didn't have to come out and say it. This was the first time he'd ever heard her talk to the man. He listened closely.

She had just started telling her husband about the supervisor when Johnny walked into Tim's cubicle and said, "Boo!"

Tim jumped. Johnny clapped his bony hands with laughter. "Sorry, sorry," he said. "Didn't mean to wake you up. How's it coming?"

"Fine."

"Liar," Johnny cackled again, and then went on to tell him that the job would probably last another five or six weeks. "Think you could stand it that long?"

"No problem," Tim said.

Johnny ripped open a Snicker's Bar, and with a mouthful asked, "What do you do in the real world?"

Tim heard Monica laugh from the other side of the wall. He wondered what her husband had said to her. When he noticed Johnny was staring at him, waiting for an answer to a question he didn't exactly remember, he said, "What do you mean?"

"You know, what are your plans? Do you go to college?"

"No."

"Any plans to go?"

"No."

"Well hell, Tim, what do you want to be when you grow up?"

Tim shrugged his shoulders. "I'm doing okay temping. They say it'll lead to a full-time job."

"Yeah, but doing what?"

"Whatever."

Johnny was picking a peanut from his teeth. "There's nothing but shit work to be found around here. A young guy like you should get out and see some of the world."

Tim focused on checking surveys, hoping Johnny would leave. It was impossible to hear Monica with all this commotion going on.

"Are you from Butler?" Johnny wanted to know.

"Cherry Run."

"Man, living in Cherry Run and waiting for the first full-time job that opens up? You must be a glutton for punishment."

Tim kept his attention on the surveys until Johnny finally stopped running at the mouth and left. He heard the zip of Monica's leather bag and the swish of her arms slipping into her coat. She was leaving for the day. Johnny had interrupted their time together. He wasn't ready to say good-bye to her yet. Recklessly, Tim jumped up, stood on his chair, and peeked over the top of the cubicle.

Monica didn't see him. But he saw her as she was leaving her cubicle. She wore a gray coat, a skirt, had blonde hair. Long, blonde hair, she had, just as he knew she would.

He sunk back down into his chair. He closed his eyes and listened. The building was quiet now. He listened to her heels clicking on the floor through the maze, until the distant tapping had disappeared. He imagined her going outside into the cold night and scraping the frost off of her car. Some sporty-looking car, he imagined. He could see her crawling inside. Her skirt gaping open, and then closing as she slid behind the wheel. Her behind sitting on the cold seat. Her warm breath fogging the windows.

Tim was getting to know his way around the building. His excursions to the men's room and break area went right past Monica's cubicle. Three times every shift, wearing tennis shoes so as not to make any unnecessary noise, he walked by and looked in. The first trip was just before Monica left for the day, and offered another glimpse at the back of her pretty head. The second and third times, after she had gone, gave him the luxury of walking more slowly, looking more closely.

On many occasions, after the full-timers had gone, he'd step inside her cubicle. He touched the chair that held her body, and once, delicately, he sat in it, seeing his reflection in the computer screen that every day reflected her face. His favorite item was a picture in a silver frame that sat above her computer. Monica stared out at him from the picture as radiantly as he had imagined her. There was a man in the picture with her. Her husband, Tim assumed. He was very plain. They seemed incompatible.

One day in the late afternoon, while Monica and her co-workers were discussing horoscopes, it came out that she was expecting a birthday in two weeks. On the eleventh. They teased her about getting to be an old working stiff, and she jokingly threw them out of her office.

Tim smiled, because he knew she had mentioned the date on purpose. This was her first major job since college. A small celebration was very important to her.

The day before her birthday, on Tim's third trip of the night, he walked into Monica's office. He gingerly took strips of purple, silver, and gold tinsel from his pockets. Carefully, he scattered them over her chair and computer. He hung a bunch over the picture, covering the face of her husband.

He looked at what he had created. Someday, he felt sure, they would laugh about this. She would say how surprised she had been, and would then tell the story to her friends as a testimony to how romantic her *new* husband could be.

When Tim went back to his cubicle, Johnny was waiting for him. "Hey man," Johnny said. "Everything okay?"

"Yes," Tim said. "I just went to the rest room."

Johnny told Tim that everything was on schedule. The job would be complete in a week and a half. "I'll recommend you for the next large order that comes in, if you're interested," Johnny said. "You know, if you haven't found full-time work anywhere."

"No problem."

"'No problem,'" Johnny imitated. "You crack me up."

By the time Tim arrived the next day, the big surprise was long over, of course. Still, he listened closely to see if he might hear mention of it. Monica was in a good mood. A few of her colleagues were talking with her when she was called out of her office for a moment.

"Come on, Linda," one voice whispered. "Was it you?"

"I swear," the woman said. "I feel terrible, but I forgot totally."

"Well, who was it?"

"Could it have been her husband?"

Tim wanted to shout, "It was me!" He hoped her husband would not get the credit for it. That man could never come up with such a nice surprise. Someday, credit would go to the rightful person, Tim thought. He could wait. All that really mattered was that Monica was made happy by the gesture. At this point, it wasn't important for Monica to know that her friends had forgotten her.

Toward the end of the fifth week, a Thursday, Monica worked late. It would be the perfect time for her to meet him. On his second trip of the night he would say hello to her. Perhaps he'd start a conversation by saying, "Someone's working late, I see," or "Well, it's nice to have company on this end of the building for a change." Then she would say something about her workload, and maybe they would start to joke about the office. He might even ask her to have a cup of coffee with him over his lunch break. They would have a nice talk, and later, maybe the next time they sat down together, the discussion would get a bit more personal.

She probably needed someone to talk with about her marriage. It's not the kind of thing she could really talk to her colleagues about. Tim would understand. He would listen, and not be judgmental. There would be the attraction between them, of course. It would be in the air when they sat next to each other, or when they happened, inadvertently, to touch.

Still, they would not let it become an issue or let it cloud their friendship. Monica was a woman of high moral standards, and he would not want to tempt her, in any way, to betray herself. It would be addressed later, after things with her husband were settled. Then there could be soft touches and playful kisses.

Finally, when the time was right, he walked out of his cubicle, around the maze, and took a deep breath as the opening to her station approached. As nonchalantly as possible, he looked in. She was sitting at the computer. Her legs were tucked underneath her. Her skirt was draped over the chair. Her shoes were off, lying next to her desk.

Tim kept moving. He passed right on to the men's room, where he took a deep breath. He needed a moment. He looked in the mirror and smiled. "Working late?" he said. The smile was too big. He tried again. "Hi, my name's Tim." He stepped away from the mirror and thought of Monica sitting at her desk. It was so adorable, the way she could kick back and relax when it was just the two of them in this part of the building.

He was very nonchalant again as he approached her cubicle, and was just about to say his line when he saw that her chair was empty. She wasn't there. He looked around. He listened for footsteps. Nothing. He should keep going, save it for the third trip, but he couldn't. He saw her shoes—long, slender, high-heeled shoes, the shoes of a woman—and he stepped inside. A breath of perfume was there. Her chair was still warm.

He looked toward the door. No one was there. Just him in her space, feeling the attraction between them. He was in love, he knew. He picked up a shoe and rubbed his fingers inside it.

"Excuse me," Monica said, and he turned around. "What are you doing?"

Monica was looking right at him, speaking in a different voice, looking with different eyes. Not smiling, like in the picture. Hard eyes. Bothered, annoyed eyes. He couldn't remember the question he was going to ask her. There was so much silence and God, oh God, he was still holding her shoe. She looked at it in his hands, and her eyes went to his temporary name tag and then back to his face.

"Who's your supervisor?" she asked, and it was like a threat. How could she threaten him? Tim could not speak, could not say a word. Nothing. Her voice had become hateful. She said again, "Who is your supervisor?" and Tim squeezed her shoe, stepping toward her to explain.

She stepped away.

Tim was terribly ashamed. Monica was gone. She was off to find Johnny. When she did, everything would be over. He had no right to be in there. He had no business touching her personal belongings. He had no right, except that he loved her, and that would be impossible to explain to other people. They never understood.

Could he say he was lost? Could he come up with a business question? No, no. She would think of him as some sort of weirdo. She must already think, how could she not think that he was some sort of maniac in her office, holding her shoe, saying nothing when she asked him a simple question? He couldn't bear the thought of Johnny questioning him as she looked on. Maybe he would call security, or the cops, and it would be a big mess that people would always talk about when they talked about him.

He felt himself running through the maze. Needing to get out. When he neared the entrance, he slowed down, nodded to the security guard—thank God Monica did not think to come to him first—and he went out into the night. He started his car and began to drive. There was no time to scrape off the windows; the defroster blew cold air. His heart was pounding. He was running for his life. There was a violent jerk, and a little cry was shaken from Tim's chest.

He had hit a parked car. And it was a newer car. Why, why, why? What was the matter with him? Now he'd done it, now he'd really done it, and they would all be after him.

He sped out of the parking lot, nearly hitting a snowy bank as he slid onto the highway. "Please, please, please," he said. The speedometer read seventy. He slowed down. Cops. He couldn't get stopped for speeding. "Breathe normally," he whispered.

The sweat on his forehead was cold. His coat. He had left his coat. The thought sent chills all over him. He had to think. What was in the coat? Right pocket: nothing. Concentrate. Left pocket: candy wrappers. The inside pocket was easy: Lifesavers and tissues. Nothing with his name on it. That was good. He could let the coat go. They could keep the last paycheck, too. It didn't matter, as long as he could have his life back. As long as he could be quiet and alone and warm in his apartment.

He calmed a bit as he drove around the turns, up and down the familiar hills. All was silent and dark outside of Butler. The windows were clear now. The car was warm. There was just the sound of the tires crunching on the layer of ash that had been scattered over the main roads. It was comforting to imagine that sound echoing through the shadowy forests and black fields of the night.

He parked behind his apartment, which sat above Hardy's TV Repair. All of the streets were empty. Cherry Run turned in extra early on winter nights. That was good.

He looked at the left front fender of his car. It wasn't nearly as bad as he'd expected. There was a slight dent and two light scratches. No one would see it unless they were looking for it. He wrapped his arms tightly around himself and started to run, and then thought he should walk to his door.

The air was bitter. So was the image of Monica's face inside his chest. It hurt. Her pretty face was not meant to be so hard and unloving. She hated him. She would tell her husband about the crazy man in her office. Her husband would comfort her, threaten to go after Tim, and then she would calm him down, telling her husband that the pervert wasn't worth it.

A pervert. That is what she must have been thinking when she stepped away from him. Did she think he would hurt her?

The musty smell of old wood and the creaking steps told him that he was home where it was safe. He locked the door, and without turning the lights on, sat at the kitchen table. He put his face in his hands. Finally, he could let it go. He cried softly over the loss of Monica, and his job, and even his freedom if they ever found out it was he who had rammed a parked car and ran. The thick wet sobs sounded to him like a sick animal. He tasted a salty tear that slid into his mouth.

Then it was quiet. He unhooked the telephone. He took the covers from his bed and wrapped himself in them. He boiled water in a pan, mesmerized by the blue flame from the stove in the dark kitchen. He poured the boiling water into a cup with a tea bag and sipped it.

Things were better already. He camped out on the couch. It seemed safer there. He lay on his side with his knees pulled up toward his chest and pulled the heavy blankets over his head.

He thought of Monica. Sweet, sweet Monica. He held her in his mind underneath the covers. She would always be with him like this. It would have to be enough.

Things were going to be fine. Really okay. There was food in the cupboards. He could stay here for a long, long time if he had to. Being quiet.

And they would forget. They would move on to the next thing and forget.

Tim could start all over again.

No problem.

THE SMELL OF SNOW

Rose was the driver because she had the better eyesight of the two. They had just finished a nice dinner at Sis's Place in Cherry Run and were on their way home. Their 1971 Chevy Impala crept down the Lawsonham hill, perfectly preserved and fully functional.

"I don't recognize this at all," she said to her husband.

"Nope," he said.

"What do I do?"

He shrugged his shoulders and scratched his thick white hair. "Keep going, I guess. Maybe it'll come to us."

"Well, it's getting dark," she said, "and we don't have a whole lot of gas."

They drove in silence.

The hill was long and winding and seemed to go deeper and deeper into the forest. "I don't know about this," Rose said. "I hope you know where you're going."

"You're the driver," Charlie said.

"So, you're the man."

Charlie looked at her and shook his head. Then he pointed out the window, "There's some people. Pull up next to them and I'll ask directions."

The teenaged boy and girl stopped walking when the car pulled up next to them. Charlie opened the door. The girl came over and smiled. "Hi Charlie!" she said, and peeked inside the car. "Hello Rose."

Rose said hello to the girl. Charlie said, "We seem to have lost our way."

The girl looked at the boy, concerned.

Charlie asked, "Do you know where we live?"

The girl said, "Cherry Run. You live on Main Street in Cherry Run."

"That sounds right," Rose said. "Ask her where we're at now."

The girl said, "You're in Lawsonham. You want to turn around and go straight back up over the hill. Just stay on the road until you come to the red light in Rimersburg. Go straight at the light and about four miles after that, you'll come right onto Main Street in Cherry Run."

The girl offered to drive them, but they assured her that they were fine now. Charlie thanked the girl and shut the door. Rose pulled the big car slowly out onto the road. A pick-up truck came around the turn and squealed to a stop just a few feet behind the Impala.

"My oh my," Rose said. "He could have run right into us."

Charlie turned around and gave the guy the dirty looks as they drove away.

"We should get something to eat," Charlie said.

"We just ate."

"We did?"

"I think so."

"May as well save the money then."

When they came to the red light in Rimersburg, Rose said, "Which way?"

Charlie looked both ways and pointed right. It began to snow.

"Oh, isn't it beautiful?" she said. "The first snow of the year. I love the first snow of the year."

She wound down the window and inhaled through her nose.

"What in the world are you doing?"

"Smelling the snow."

"Good gravy, if I told you once, I told you a million times, snow don't have a smell."

"Oh yes it does. I remember—"

"Put that window up, and I mean now!"

Rose rolled the window up. "You don't need to be mean about it."

"I'm not being mean for heaven's sake, but I'm not going to catch my death just because you want to smell the snow."

Rose mumbled, "There is no reason to snap at a person. And snow most certainly does have a smell."

Charlie was tinkering with the heater. Rose continued, "Snow smells cold and very fresh. Almost sweet this time of year. By the end of winter, it has more of a sharp, stinging smell. My dad could tell what month it was by the scent of a snowfall."

Air blasted out of the dash. Charlie smiled. "There we go."

"That's cold air."

"Well, give it a chance, why don't ya?"

Charlie stared at the dash and Rose watched the road. "You growl at me for putting down the window and you blast cold air through the car. It's still cold, so it is."

Charlie fiddled with the levers until the fan began to blow warm air. "There we go. That's more like it."

"The smell of sassafras tea goes very well with the smell of snow," Rose said. "I grew up with that smell. That's why I always keep a pot of it on the stove all winter."

"There hasn't been a pot of it on the stove for a long time."

"We'd go out and dig up the sassafras roots in the late fall and put them in bags. Hang the bags in the cellar."

"We haven't had sassafras in a dog's age. Two or three dog's ages."

"Edward took his with honey. He sure loved it, didn't he though?"

"Edward," Charlie said, closing his eyes to see the boy. "Edward."

"God blessed us with that one, so He did."

"Damned army," Charlie said under his breath.

"I can see him like it was yesterday."

"Army says this, army says that."

"Just as handsome as could be."

"I don't know how anyone could believe a word the army says."

"And kind. Even when he was little, there was a gentleness to him."

Charlie stared out of the window.

"'Whosoever believeth in Him shall never perish, but have everlasting life,'" Rose said and nodded.

They drove in silence.

"Do you know where in the world you're going?"

"I'm going home," she said. "Trying, anyway." Then she looked at the gas gauge. "Merciful heaven, is that right?"

"Is what right?"

"Are we almost out of gas?"

Charlie leaned over and looked at the gauge. "We'll pull off at the next station."

The next station was the General Store in Sligo. They drove over the bell and waited for the attendant. "Maybe this is one of those places where a person has to serve themselves," Rose said.

Charlie was about to open the door when a kid with long, straggly hair came out. "How much?"

Rose wound down the window. She smiled at the boy. "Fill it, please."

"Put that window up," Charlie said.

"I'm going to have to put it right back down again in a couple of minutes."

"So, why freeze till then?"

Rose rolled up the window. "Did you ever try to smell the snow?"

"Huh?"

"You're always saying the snow don't have a smell, but did you ever *try* to smell it?"

"Of all the crazy things to ask a guy."

"I'll bet you never tried."

The attendant came to the driver's window, and Rose made a big show of winding it down again. "Twenty-four even," he said.

Charlie handed the kid the twenty dollar bill from his wallet. The boy stood there for a moment and cleared his throat. "Ah, I need four more dollars."

Charlie leaned over and looked at the boy. "You need what?"

"It's twenty-four dollars. You only gave me twenty."

Charlie looked into his empty wallet. "You need how much more?"

"Four more dollars," the kid said, then added, "sir."

"That's awfully dear, isn't it?"

The kid shrugged his shoulders. "We're a little more expensive than the other places around, but not much."

Charlie said to Rose in a low voice, "Do you have anything?"

"No. Where would I get any money?"

Charlie opened his door and went to the back of the car. He motioned for the kid to join him. "How short am I?"

"Four dollars."

Charlie shook his head. "Well, I don't have any more cash on me now. But I'm good for it." He took off his watch and handed it to the kid. "You keep this as insurance until I come back."

"That's not necessary," the kid said.

"No sir," Charlie said. "You put that in your cash box and I'll trade you four dollars for it tomorrow."

"Thank you."

"No, thank *you*."

When Charlie got back into the car, Rose said, "Is everything okay?"

"All square."

At the yellow blinker in Sligo, Rose asked, "Which way?"

Charlie looked both ways and pointed right.

"I've got to get my hair done," Rose said.

As they passed the Curlsville road, Charlie said, "Now that looks familiar."

Rose started to slow down. "Should we go that way?"

A horn blasted from the car behind them.

"Pull off," Charlie said. "Let that idiot pass."

She did, and both of them gave the guy very dirty looks. "Should I turn around?"

"No. I don't think it was anything. Keep going straight."

Curlsville was where Charlie lived until he was twelve years old. He used to buy sugar and flour for his mother at the town market and would fish in the creek that ran next to it. Strip-mining had long ago poisoned the water with sulfur, and all that remained of the town market was its stone foundation.

By the time they reached Clarion, half an hour later, it was dark. There was two inches of snow already on the ground, and it was coming down even faster now. When Rose tried to stop at the red light in Clarion, their car slid and almost bumped a car parked along the street.

"Don't hit the brake like that!" Charlie yelled. "Pump the brakes. Pump them."

Rose's experience with winter driving was minimal. They never went out when it was bad. And even though Rose was a cautious driver, she hadn't started driving until she was already considered an old woman. Like a lot of area women from her generation, there was no need for her to have a license. Her work was in the home, or within walking distance of it, and Charlie always drove when they went shopping or to town. At least, he did until his eyes deteriorated to a point that his doctor (and the state) insisted that he no longer drive.

Rose had been the prize pupil in the Driver's Ed. class at Cherry Run High School. The kids loved her and called her Grandma. When she took her test with the state cop in the passenger seat, ten teenagers came out for moral support, and every one of them was crossing their fingers or holding their breath. When they returned, the old cop took his time filling out papers and checking this and that, and finally stamped the papers and handed them to Rose.

"Did you pass?" one of the kids asked as Rose walked over to them.

She was studying the papers. "I'm not sure."

They all huddled around her, searching the forms. "Right there, she passed!" And a cheer went up as though the Cherry Run Raiders had scored a winning touchdown.

"Those kids were so sweet," Rose said.

"Huh?"

"Those kids. They sure made me feel at home."

Charlie didn't know what she was talking about and was too worried about the weather to ask a second time. They went straight at the light in Clarion. As they were going down the Clarion River hill, they could see nothing but snow pouring into their field of vision. No road, no trees, nothing but snow. A whiteout.

"I can't see the road," Rose said.

Charlie leaned forward in his seat as though that would bring a clearer picture to his weak vision. "We're going too fast down over here."

But every time Rose pushed the brakes the car would slide, picking up speed.

"Pump the brakes," Charlie said.

It was at this moment that Clarion, the red light, and the steep hill re-emerged in Charlie's mind. "The river hill," he said.

"I don't know what to do," Rose said.

Charlie realized that at the bottom of this hill was the river. If they began to slide, they would either hit the bridge or plunge into the water. The ditch seemed like the best place to go.

"Cut the wheels," he said, "to the right."

Rose did what her husband said, but the car began to skid. "What do I do?"

Before Charlie could answer, instinct took over and Rose pushed the brake. The car moved broadside down the hill like a giant sled, faster and faster until there was a terrible jolt.

Then, silence.

"Are you okay?" Charlie asked.

Rose was crying. "I'm sorry, Charlie."

"No. It wasn't your fault. It was the damn weather. The damn snow."

"I'm sorry," she said.

They had hit the bank on the opposite side of the road and were deep in the ditch. "Are you okay?"

"I think so," Rose whimpered.

"Dry up now. It wasn't your fault. We're okay and the car can be fixed."

Charlie got out of the car and looked at it. He said, "Climb out my side. We'll have to walk."

It was difficult for Rose to move across the seat. When she got out, she nearly fell, saving herself by grabbing onto Charlie's shoulder and the open car door. The moment she let go of them, she did fall.

"Good God," Charlie said as he tried to help her stand.

"It's my shoes," she said.

Charlie noticed that they were dress shoes with heels. "You can't walk in those."

"I know I can't," Rose said. He guided her to the edge of the seat and she sat down.

Charlie was already covered with snow. He looked at the river, no more than thirty yards away. He looked at the steep white hill in the dark night. "You stay here," he said. "I'll walk for help."

"Oh, I don't know," Rose said.

"If I can find someone with one of those four-wheel drives, they could come down here easy and drive us home," he said. "Get in there. Shut the door. It won't take long."

"You can't walk in this by yourself."

"Sure I can. I've walked through a lot worse. Go on, get in there and shut the door before there's not a bit of heat left."

"Well…"

"Come on now."

Rose pulled her legs inside the car. Charlie went to shut the door when she said, "Gimme a kiss before you go."

"For cripe's sake, I'm only going up over the hill."

"Well, give me one anyway."

Charlie leaned his cheek toward Rose, and she kissed him.

He pulled his coat tightly around himself, flipped up the collar, and began walking up the hill.

Clouds of snow swirled and spun through the tall, dark trees on the Clarion River hill. Town was a long mile away for an old man with small steps. The cold wind stung his sinuses and made his ears burn. The snow gathered everywhere and turned everything white, even the air. It laid on his shoulders, it stuck to his pants, and even a young man would have had difficulty walking through it.

The constant downpour of snow on the deserted hill was hypnotizing. Only the tracks of the Impala marked the hill, and they were disappearing quickly. Before long, Charlie forgot where it was that he was going. It had something to do with Rose, he knew, and it was very important that he get there.

His memory had been doing this to him for the past few years. He found it terribly frustrating. If a guy was going to start going nuts, Charlie figured, he should go all the way nuts. This bit of getting things right half of the time and ending up lost half of the time was for the birds.

Even though he could not remember where he was going or exactly why, he was remembering, as if it were yesterday, that afternoon in 1944 when it snowed very much like it was snowing now. He'd just fired the furnace and was about to do some shoveling when he heard the preacher knocking on their front door. The preacher was a nice enough guy, and Rose thought a lot of him, but Charlie found the guy very dry and hard to listen to.

But the reverend wasn't on a social call that day. He had something to tell them. Some news. Not good news. Rose had poured them each a cup of coffee. Charlie remembered how the coffee grew cold and how the three cups sat untouched on the kitchen table for days. The reverend told them that their boy, their only boy, Edward, was a hero, a man who had served his country, a man who did what was asked of him, and as a result, had made the ultimate sacrifice.

For the first and last time in his adult life, Charlie wept out loud. And Rose with him. Their life, in that instant, had changed forever. In the last letter the boy had sent, he'd said he was coming home. He said he was going to eat Rose's cooking until it was coming out of his ears. He said he wanted to find a job with Charlie so they could work together like they did before the war took him away. He said he couldn't wait to go hunting again with Charlie. "A guy really misses stuff like that," the boy wrote.

The letter was still in Charlie's wallet. All that remained of it was a handful of crumbled pieces. Even though the penciled words had entirely vanished, Charlie knew every word of the letter. He could still see the boy's handwriting, sloppy like his dad's, as if it were still visible.

For the first few years, they referred to the incident simply as "the tragedy." Charlie would often say that until a person loses a child, they have not felt the worst life has to offer. "Parents we expect to lose, even brothers and sisters in time," Charlie said. "But never our children, not ever our babies."

Rose had nightmares for months afterward. Charlie began to fear for her sanity. The only relief she found was in church. She had always been a church-going woman, and they had brought Edward up a Christian, but after the tragedy, she went to every available service at the Cherry Run Church—five times a week. But even more important than the church or the people was the fact that, through this terrible thing, Rose had found something of her own. Something that doctors and friends and even Charlie could not give her: prayer. Charlie was glad that she had found something to pull her through.

Charlie, however, did not find any comfort in prayer. In fact, as Rose started going to church all of the time, Charlie stopped altogether. When he tried to go, he felt like a hypocrite. He was stuck between feeling that there was no God, and that if there was, He was not fair, and surely not good. Either way, the feeling made him uncomfortable around church-going people. He didn't want to hear that his son's death was "meant to be" or that he was "with God now."

It was five years after the preacher's visit that the government sent the casket back to Cherry Run from Japan. The casket was laid in the back room of Charlie and Rose's house. A picture of the boy was placed on top of it.

"It could be anybody in that box," Charlie said to the friends and family who had come to pay their respects. No one knew what to say to that.

There was always a part of Charlie that believed he would see his boy again. Part of him knew that the preacher was wrong, the army was wrong, that his boy was not at all dead, and that one day he would come up the road waving his arms, crying out to them that it had all been a big mistake. He had read and heard of many mix-ups in the army's red tape. It could be that Edward was lost and hurt, crossing continents and seas to get back home to Cherry Run.

Finally, the lights of Clarion were coming into focus through the heavy snowfall. And that was not all. There was someone walking down the hill toward him. A tall, thin man, and Charlie could tell by his walk, a young one. It was a familiar walk, too. Charlie's heart began to race as the young man began to wave his arms and run toward him.

"Edward," he whispered, as the boy came closer.

Back at the car, the windows were covered with snow, so inside things were dark, noiseless, still. Rose sat quietly and wondered how much snow was covering her. Earlier, she was unsuccessful in her attempts to start the engine for heat. Now, cold under her clothes, she was beginning to feel frightened. She wound the window down a bit, and heavy clumps of snow fell inside on the seat. She cried, "Charlie! Charlie!" but heard only the wind. Again she called, "Charlie! Charlie!" and then wound the window up.

Charlie always took care of her. Even when he grumbled about it, he protected her. He was a good provider, she was proud to say. Her two sisters weren't so lucky. Their men liked to drink, and both of them, *both* of them were known to visit the cathouse in Cherry Run before it was finally shut down for good. That place saw many family paychecks handed over to painted women who played on a man's weakness. Her sisters would never admit it, and Rose would never let on, but they all knew. The whole town knew.

Rose closed her eyes and folded her hands and bowed her head. There was one thing she'd had longer than she'd had Charlie, in good times and bad times and all times, and that was prayer. She'd had prayer ever since she was a little girl.

"Dear Lord," she said aloud, "I, Rose, come before you tonight." This was the way her mother taught her to start every prayer when she was a little girl. Even when she really learned to pray, after the loss of Edward, when prayer was all that held her together through the nightmares and the unspeakable pain, Rose started each prayer that way.

There were so many things in this old world, Rose knew, that a person, especially a woman, could do nothing about. No matter how clean she kept her house, no matter how good she was about making meals out of whatever was available, no matter how much she loved and took care of her husband and her baby, no matter how nice she was to the neighbors, and no matter how much she helped out at the church, she could never stop wars, or keep her baby from dying, or stop Charlie from getting sick, or change a single, horrible thing on the nightly news. In all of those things and so many others, Rose was helpless.

But God was not. Prayer was always worthwhile. It was always important. There could never be too much prayer. Sometimes even the President would ask the people to pray, and Rose took that request, from several Presidents, very seriously. Because she could always pray. And prayer never failed to comfort her.

Rose prayed for Charlie. She prayed and prayed for him. She prayed for Charlie until she was sure the Lord was with him, but she didn't want to stop there. She no longer needed to pray for herself. Just by listening, God had already taken care of her. She was feeling very comfortable and warm, wonderfully warm. So she prayed for all of the people in the world, especially for the ones who didn't have prayer. Those who were lost. Those who didn't know how to pray, and those who had no one to pray for them. The ones who do the awful things that get reported on the nightly news and the crazy ones and the painted ladies like the ones that used to work in Cherry Run who surely must have come from bad homes and had no one praying for them.

When Rose had prayed for everyone she could think of, she opened her eyes. For reasons she could not explain, it did not surprise her to see Jesus on the seat beside her, even though she'd never seen him before, and even though he looked nothing like he did in the pictures with the robe and the beard and the long hair. His face was beyond any comparison, but it was beautiful. And then there were his eyes: the perfect color for eyes, but a color she could not identify. A *new* color. Looking into His eyes allowed her a capacity for joy that reached beyond every boundary, raced through her body, surged through her brain, and transcended her faith.

Jesus smiled at Rose.

She had a lifetime of things to say and questions to ask, and she did, instantly, and was answered, instantly, all without speaking a single word.

It tickled her, also, when Jesus told her that he, too, enjoyed the smell of a fresh snowfall.

Charlie often imagined what he would do if his boy did come home to him. He imagined that he would throw his arms around his son and hug him and kiss him, even though that kind of affection was never his way. But he was sure it would be the only way to show how happy he would be.

But now that his boy was before him, here on the Clarion River hill, in the midst of a snowstorm, Charlie could only stare in wonder at the handsome young man.

"Dad," the boy said and put out his hand. Charlie took the boy's hand in his own and then pulled him into the tightest hug he was sure he had ever given anyone.

"I missed you, son. I missed you something fierce." And with that, for the second time in his adult life, Charlie cried.

"I missed you, too," the boy said. "I couldn't wait to get home."

"You look the same," Charlie said. "Maybe a little bigger. But the same."

"You too, Dad."

"I knew they were wrong," he said. "I want you to know that I never believed it. Your mother...it broke her heart. But I knew you'd be back. Damn army messes everything up. Your mother, we have to go tell her, right now."

"Okay."

"Let's go."

"Lead the way."

Charlie looked in both directions and then focused his eyes down the hill. "We hit a bank. Car's stuck. You and me together though, we can push it out."

"Sure. The two of us, together, will have no problem. Remember the time we had to push that big old Ford of Uncle Bobby's out of the drainage ditch?"

"Darn right I remember. Ruined a perfectly good pair of pants over that one."

"Uncle Bobby was always showing off for the ladies."

"Yeah, and always making a horse's ass of himself. Your mother got all the brains in that family."

"How's the work situation?"

"I'm retired now. Have been for a long, long time."

"I was hoping we could get on somewhere together like we did before all this army business."

"I'd like that."

"I remember, after work in the wintertime, Mom always had a pot of sassafras tea waiting for us. Man, nothing tasted better after crawling out of those cold, dark mines."

"Mines are all closed down, now."

"Well, I guess that's not too much of a shame."

"No. Hard work. Dangerous. Don't know how I did it all those years."

"We'll find something better than mining."

"Sure we will. God, I'm glad you're home, boy. I never believed it. I always said, 'One of these days that boy is going to come right up the road, waving his arms and hooting and hollering, like the good old days.'"

The boy stopped. The snow laid softly in his dark hair. His eyes were full of wonder. "I can hear the river," he said. He walked to an old tree and sat at the bottom of it. "It's so good to be home. I really missed home."

"Don't need to sit on my account," Charlie said. "I can keep going. I'm not *that* old."

"I know," Edward said. "I remember hunting. You could out-tramp anyone. Always could." Edward opened his mouth and stuck his tongue out to catch snowflakes. "Mmm, snow tastes good this time of year."

"Good gravy, you sound as crazy as your mother. Your mother…we have to get to her."

"She's okay, Dad."

"Are you sure?"

"I'm sure."

"It broke her heart. There was nothing anyone could do."

"Mom's okay now, Dad. She's in good shape." The boy laughed, "So Mom's still eating snowflakes, huh?"

"And smelling them," Charlie said. "That woman insists they have a smell. Her dad, your granddad, was the same way."

"Are you sure they don't have a smell?" Edward inhaled through his nose. "I don't know. The air never seems to smell like that unless it's snowing."

Charlie looked up at the millions of white flakes dropping from the black sky. He took a whiff. He looked puzzled and sniffed again, deeply this time. "By jumpings…" He inhaled a third time. "Well, I'll be." Charlie looked at Edward.

The boy shrugged his shoulders. "I always sided with Mom on that one."

"How in the world could I have missed it all those years?" Charlie pointed a finger at Edward. "If you mention this to your mother, I'll never hear the end of it."

"I won't say a word," Edward said, "…if you'll sit with me for a while."

Charlie looked down the hill.

"It's okay," Edward said. "Honest."

"Well, maybe for a minute," Charlie said, and sat next to his boy in the snow, beneath the giant oak tree.

Edward had some ideas about where to hunt this year. He said he had a feeling that one of them was going to drop a trophy buck this season. "Do you remember the first time you took me out?"

"Course I do."

"You said I was all hat and boots."

Charlie laughed. "It was true. That's all I could see trudging along behind me. Your mother was watching out the window, just laughing and shaking her head."

"Those were good times."

"The best."

The wind quieted.

Silently, the snow, smelling fresh and clean, covered their tracks.

THE FOURTH OPTION

When trying to pee a word in the snow, or in Seth's case, an entire phrase, there is very little time to ponder. He dallied too long at the start and, as a result, ran out of fuel before he'd finished the first word. He jiggled a bit, but there was no use.

"Sure enough," Seth said aloud. "That's what a guy gets for lingering." He looked out over the snow-covered hills of the strip cuts and shouted to the lights of Cherry Run below, "Life is too short to linger. When you've got to go, you've got to go."

Then he zipped up.

This was the first time he'd ever been drunk. At twenty-one, he had to admit he'd held out pretty well; the town didn't offer much else in the way of entertainment. Still, he was sure it was a bad sign. Drinking was just the kind of thing that could make hanging around a little longer seem bearable.

Seth knew better. He didn't belong here. Never did. He needed to see new things and talk to different people and meet women who wanted to do something other than get married and have babies. Cherry Run was just not the place for a guy with big dreams. He'd figured that out by the time he was fourteen years old, but wanting to go and actually going were two different things. His big mistake was assuming that there would be someone or something to point the way, to give him direction.

There wasn't.

Which is not to say there weren't plenty of people telling him to be realistic and to grow up and to be thankful for his job at Lyndora Business Forms. When these people got going, shaking their heads at him, he knew there was no point in trying to describe the images in his head of being a writer, blazing a trail across America, seeing things, having adventures and writing books about it all. And yet, not being able to express it was pushing him over the edge. He had reached a point where he simply could not breathe and if he stayed any longer, some part of him—the best part of him, he was sure—would die.

Something had to be done. There could be no more dawdling. He concluded that there were four ways out and the older a person got, the less likely they were to apply any of them.

Earlier that evening, he'd found himself trying to explain these four options to the regulars at the Ruffled Grouse, who were so entertained by seeing a nondrinker get drunk that they made sure Seth didn't have to pay for a single beer. They all laughed when he told them the stuff tasted awful, and laughed even harder when, after his third one, he told them the taste was starting to grow on him.

Feeling very relaxed, he decided to take the opportunity to try as many different brands of beer as possible. Seth got quite a kick out of asking for a Bud or an Iron or a Rock or a Ribbon like one of the guys. After a while, everyone in the place seemed like his good buddy, and he couldn't stop talking to them about everything. Then, out of nowhere, the whole world began to move in slow motion, and Seth knew it was time to go.

A few guys offered to drive him home, telling him he was in no shape to drive. But he had no intention of driving. He wanted to walk. In fact, the only thing he really liked about living in Cherry Run was walking through the woods and strip cuts that surrounded it. Especially at night.

As he was going out the door, a large, hairy guy he vaguely knew as Mike from Lyndora Business Forms stopped him. "Are you sure you're okay?" he asked.

"Yeah," Seth said, "I want to walk."

Mike had been at the bar all night listening to Seth rattle on about options, but hadn't said a word. The big man looked at him very seriously and said, "My vote, whatever it's worth, is to take the fourth option. Take it and don't look back." Then he slapped him hard on the back and Seth continued out the door.

The night was a real beauty. The moon was full and so bright that he could see his shadow. He went into the woods at the edge of town where he contemplated the clear, silent sky and glittering snow that clung to the trees and covered the ground unbroken and undisturbed. Then Seth Hardy began to run, dodging low-hanging branches and hopping over fallen trees, letting his instincts take over, imagining himself to be a deer, then a coyote. His mind spun until all thoughts disappeared. He moved effortlessly through the dark forest until he came to the sulfur stream. Even then, without slowing down, he took a wild leap that carried him to the other side. His landing, however, was less graceful. He ended up face first in the snow, which led him to the conclusion that he had better walk for a while.

Crunching and snapping his way through the snowy leaves and brittle sticks, Seth decided that this getting drunk business wasn't so bad. He could understand now why people did it so often and concluded that it was a good thing he hadn't discovered it before. He wasn't sure if he'd ever do it again, but tonight it was fun, and he wanted to hold on to the feeling as long as he could. When the woods gave way to the emptiness of the strip cuts, he stopped at the forest's edge and noticed that the spoil piles had become beautiful. Strip-mined decades ago and left for dead, the hills were normally stark and black and lifeless, with the exception of a few pine trees and a smattering of weeds. But tonight, covered by an immaculate layer of snow, they glistened in the blue light of the moon like piles of precious gems.

The tallest and steepest one of the bunch was Seth's favorite, though he'd never seen it look the way it did tonight. During the summer, the motorcycle-riding teenagers of the area liked to climb it to show off the power of their dirt bikes. It was known among them as BFH: Big Fucking Hill. To Seth it had always been something different. It was a place he had come to many times in the past, and climbed to the top of to sit and think. When he was up there, looking down, every worry, every thought, every fear seemed manageable.

He again thought of his options and, as before, concluded that there were only four ways out for a guy in his position. The first three were the most common, and certainly the most feasible.

First, a guy could move in with family or friends who lived somewhere else. Second, he could join one of the armed forces. Or third, he could go away to college.

However, Seth didn't know anyone who lived anywhere much different than Cherry Run. He had no interest in joining the armed forces. And he couldn't begin to afford to go away to college.

That left the fourth option. The one seldom used and almost always fated for failure. The simplest and most complicated one of all: *just going*. Loading up the car and going, with no plan and only instinct to follow.

Of course, there were a hundred reasons why the fourth option was the wrong way to go. He knew his mom would name all of them, and when she reached the end, she'd start over again. His dad wouldn't be in favor of it either. He'd tell him that if he kept working at Lyndora Business Forms and taking classes at Butler Community College, things would somehow work out, that maybe he could eventually save enough money to transfer to a bigger school.

But Seth hated the job at Lyndora Business Forms and had already exhausted the community college's literature and writing courses. He didn't know how he could stand a couple more days, let alone months or maybe years. According to Seth's calculations, the hundred reasons his mom would offer and the logical plans his dad would suggest were nothing more than a lot of excuses to stay where he didn't want to stay.

The BFH sparkled in the distance. Gazing at it, a strange sensation came over him and he began to do something that he hadn't done since he was a kid. He began to pray.

It started out silent, but soon he was speaking out loud. He was asking God to help him and to give him courage, and at some point, to his own surprise, he heard himself turning the prayer into a proposal. A wager with God:

"If I can run all the way to the top of that spoil pile, the biggest one around, snow and all, without stopping to rest, then You will show me how to get out of here and become an honest-to-goodness, real and true, published writer. But if I don't make it, then I'll forget the whole thing and just accept being stuck here with the rest of them."

The night was windless. Quiet. Seth began to feel that he was all alone and that he was a fool standing there with his churning stomach and hazy head waiting for an answer.

Then God said, "GO!"

And he was off, running as hard as he could, racing at full speed toward the hillside. As he made his approach, his eyes flashed to the very top and locked onto a lone pine tree that stood there. He imagined a heavy rope attached to the tree securing his climb and pulling him toward it.

The first fourth of the BFH was easy. He felt quick and strong with his legs thundering madly beneath him, but as the hill grew steeper, he began to slip and stumble. Keeping his eyes fastened to the tree, he drove his hiking boots through the crusty snow and into the coal dirt beneath. By midpoint, his progress began to slow so he pushed harder, aiming directly for the pine tree, leaning forward, pumping his arms, breathing deeply, letting the cold air stab inside his chest.

He regained a strong, steady pace until a hard patch of ice sent his feet out from under him, slamming his face into the frozen ground and sending his body sliding quickly to the bottom. "No!" he cried, and before he came to the base of the hill, he was on his feet, scaling upwards again.

His head was spinning and warm blood trickled from his nose into his open mouth. He forced himself to focus on the tree at the top of the hill, and pushed as hard as he could toward it. Approaching the icy spot again, he resolved to fight right over it this time, but he went down. Immediately, he scrambled to his hands and knees, hurling his arms against the hill, digging his fingers into the ice, flailing his legs, thrashing and writing his way over the patch.

The taste of blood made him gag and his stomach seized, but he continued for the top of the hill, growling and groaning for it, clawing with numb fingers, until he passed the ice and went on, higher and higher, standing again.

Only a couple of feet from the top, he hit another patch of ice, but managed to throw himself at the pine tree, grabbing a jagged, frosty limb before his knees went out from under him. He kicked furiously and pulled himself toward the tree. The branch cracked at the same moment that his boots dug into the ground.

With the branch coming off in his hands, Seth let out a powerful yell and threw himself for the crest of the BFH. He crawled the last few inches, struggled to his feet and skipped across the ground in a ridiculous dance of triumph.

"Whoooo!" he cried to the moon and stars, spinning around and around, laughing at himself, a drunken, bloodied fool covered in sweat and snow. "Whooooooooo!"

He stumbled to his knees, though the world kept spinning. "Okay," he said, "no more spinning, we're done spinning here now." His stomach heaved, but Seth swallowed hard and closed his eyes and whispered, "You're okay, you did it, you made it." He squeezed his eyes tightly and took long, deep breaths and told himself he would not be sick. He told himself again and again. The feeling passed. He knew he would be alright.

Seth rolled onto his back under the bright and endless sky. His breath mixed with the night air in warm puffs of steam. Like the train, he thought, like the train that chugged up the impossible hill. His heart rocked around in his chest, crazy and all the way alive. "Amen," he said, "amen."

He rubbed a handful of snow over his hot face, and pressed it to his throbbing nose until it stopped bleeding. A blissful exhaustion came over him as he slowly moved to his hunkers and looked down over the spoil pile. The lights of Cherry Run flickered like a few candles in the middle of the forest. Cocooned by a wall of hills, it was easy for a person to forget they had a choice. No one had to cling to a place, like the scattered pine trees did to the strip cuts, just because it was familiar. Once a guy got the gumption to crawl up the hills and out of the valleys and take an honest look at things, that was pretty clear.

Since he only got as far as "perspec—" before running out of pee, he finished writing his phrase in the snow with the pine tree branch:

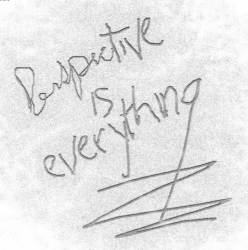

With the metallic taste of blood lingering in his mouth, he looked down over the spoil pile and noted his tracks: where he had slipped, where he had fallen, and where he had managed to dig into the dirt and drive forward. His wet clothes were starting to chill him, and not feeling too drunk anymore, he chose—just like that—the fourth option.

You are now leaving

CHERRY RUN, PENNSYLVANIA

Come again!

Photo by Eve Bregman

David Drayer is a native of western Pennsylvania. He earned a BA from the University of Pittsburgh and an MFA from the University of Iowa. He wrote, performed, and toured his one-man play, *Call of the Wolf: An Evening with Jack London* and recently co-wrote and starred in the independent film, *Sammyville*. David now lives in Los Angeles, California and is working on his second novel.

For additional copies of STRIP CUTS:

Check your favorite bookstore
or order toll-free
1-888-39-ROWDY
or
Order books directly from the publisher:

YES, I want _____ copies of STRIP CUTS at $13.95 each, plus $4 shipping for the first book and $2 for each additional book (California residents please add applicable sales tax). Please allow 15 days for delivery.

International orders must be accompanied by a postal money order in U.S. funds. Shipping and handling is $9 for the first book and $5 for each additional book. Please allow 30 days for delivery.

My check or money order for $_____ is enclosed.

Name_____

Organization_____

Address_____

City/State/Zip_____

Phone_____

E-mail_____

Please make your check payable and return to:
Rowdy House Publishing
P.O. Box 251293
Los Angeles, CA 90025

For credit card orders, call toll-free **1-888-39-ROWDY**.